First World War
and Army of Occupation
War Diary
France, Belgium and Germany

28 DIVISION
83 Infantry Brigade
East Yorkshire Regiment
2nd Battalion
15 January 1915 - 31 October 1915

WO95/2275/1

The Naval & Military Press Ltd
www.nmarchive.com
Published in association with The National Archives

Published by

The Naval & Military Press Ltd

Unit 10 Ridgewood Industrial Park,

Uckfield, East Sussex,

TN22 5QE England

Tel: +44 (0) 1825 749494

www.naval-military-press.com

www.nmarchive.com

This diary has been reprinted in facsimile from the original. Any imperfections are inevitably reproduced and the quality may fall short of modern type and cartographic standards.

© Crown Copyright
Images reproduced by permission of The National Archives, London, England, 2015.

Contents

Document type	Place/Title	Date From	Date To
Heading	WO95/2275/1		
Heading	2nd Bn East Yorks Regt Jan-Oct 1915		
Heading	2nd Battn. East Yorkshire Regiment. January 1915 (15.1.15 to 31.1.15)		
Miscellaneous	On His Majesty's Service.		
Heading	War Diary Of 2nd Battn East Yorkshire Regt From 15.1.15 To 31.1.15 Volume I		
War Diary	Winchester	15/01/1915	17/01/1915
War Diary	Meteren	18/01/1915	31/01/1915
Heading	2nd Battn East Yorkshire Regiment February 1915		
Miscellaneous	On His Majesty's Service.		
War Diary	Vlamertinghe	01/02/1915	01/02/1915
War Diary	Ypres	02/02/1915	06/02/1915
War Diary	Vlamertinghe	07/02/1915	10/02/1915
War Diary	Ypres	11/02/1915	19/02/1915
War Diary	Vlamertinghe	21/02/1915	26/02/1915
War Diary	Zillebeke	27/02/1915	28/02/1915
Heading	2nd Battn. East Yorkshire Regiment March 1915		
Miscellaneous	On His Majesty's Service.		
War Diary	Zillebeke	01/03/1915	01/03/1915
War Diary	Vlamertinghe	02/03/1915	02/03/1915
War Diary	Bailleul	03/03/1915	06/03/1915
War Diary	Neuve Eglise	07/03/1915	07/03/1915
War Diary	Wulverghem	08/03/1915	11/03/1915
War Diary	Dranoutre	12/03/1915	14/03/1915
War Diary	Bailleul	15/03/1915	16/03/1915
War Diary	Dranoutre	17/03/1915	17/03/1915
War Diary	Wulverghem	18/03/1915	23/03/1915
War Diary	Neuve Eglise	24/03/1915	28/03/1915
War Diary	Wulverghem	29/03/1915	31/03/1915
Heading	28th Division 2nd Lieut Yorkshire Regt Vol IV 1-30.4.15		
War Diary	Wulverghem	01/04/1915	02/04/1915
War Diary	Bailleul	03/04/1915	03/04/1915
War Diary	Westoutre	04/04/1915	08/04/1915
War Diary	Ypres	09/04/1915	09/04/1915
War Diary	Zonnebeke	10/04/1915	12/04/1915
War Diary	Ypres	13/04/1915	14/04/1915
War Diary	Zonnebeke	15/04/1915	19/04/1915
War Diary	Ypres	20/04/1915	22/04/1915
War Diary	St Jean	23/04/1915	27/04/1915
War Diary	Ypres	29/04/1915	30/04/1915
Heading	28th Division 2nd East Yorkshire Vol V 1-31.5.15		
Miscellaneous	3rd Echelon	24/06/1915	24/06/1915
War Diary	Ypres	01/05/1915	11/05/1915
War Diary	Poperinghe	12/05/1915	14/05/1915
War Diary	Winnezeele	15/05/1915	21/05/1915
War Diary	Ypres	22/05/1915	31/05/1915
Map			
Heading	2nd Battn. East Yorkshire Regiment June 1915		

Miscellaneous	On His Majesty's Service.		
War Diary	Ypres	01/06/1915	02/06/1915
War Diary	Vlamertinghe	03/06/1915	03/06/1915
War Diary	Winnezeele	04/06/1915	14/06/1915
War Diary	La Clytte	15/06/1915	18/06/1915
War Diary	Kemmel	19/06/1915	30/06/1915
Heading	2nd Battn. East Yorkshire Regiment. July 1915		
Miscellaneous	On His Majesty's Service.		
War Diary	Kemmel	01/07/1915	05/07/1915
War Diary	La Clytte	06/07/1915	10/07/1915
War Diary	Kemmel	11/07/1915	15/07/1915
War Diary	La Clytte	16/07/1915	16/07/1915
War Diary	Locre	17/07/1915	18/07/1915
War Diary	Wulverghem	19/07/1915	29/07/1915
War Diary	Locre	30/07/1915	31/07/1915
Heading	2nd Battn. East Yorkshire Regiment August 1915		
Miscellaneous	On His Majesty's Service.		
War Diary	Locre	01/08/1915	03/08/1915
War Diary	Scherpenberg	04/08/1915	05/08/1915
War Diary	Kemmel	06/08/1915	12/08/1915
War Diary	Scherpenberg	13/08/1915	17/08/1915
War Diary	Kemmel	18/08/1915	24/08/1915
War Diary	Scherpenberg	25/08/1915	30/08/1915
War Diary	Kemmel	31/08/1915	31/08/1915
Map			
Miscellaneous			
Heading	2nd Battn. East Yorkshire Regiment. September 1915		
Miscellaneous	On His Majesty's Service.		
Heading	Confidential. War Diary Of 2/ East Yorkshire Regt From 1st Sept 1915 To 30th Sept 1915		
War Diary	K and L Trenches	01/09/1915	04/09/1915
War Diary	Scherpenberg	05/09/1917	10/09/1917
War Diary	K & L Trenches	11/09/1915	17/09/1915
War Diary	Scherpenberg	18/09/1915	22/09/1915
War Diary	Outersteene	23/09/1915	24/09/1915
War Diary	Robecq	26/09/1915	26/09/1915
War Diary	Noyelles	27/09/1915	30/09/1915
Miscellaneous	Appendices		
Miscellaneous	A Form. Messages And Signals.		
Heading	2nd Battn. East Yorkshire Regiment. October 1915		
Miscellaneous	On His Majesty's Service.		
Miscellaneous	War Diary 2nd Bn East Yorks Regt		
Heading	War Diary Of 2nd East Yorkshire Regt From 1st October 1915 To 31st October 1915		
War Diary	Near Hulluch	01/10/1915	01/10/1915
War Diary	Annequin	02/10/1915	02/10/1915
War Diary	Near Hulluch	03/10/1915	05/10/1915
War Diary	Annequin	06/10/1915	06/10/1915
War Diary	Ales Harisoirs	07/10/1915	14/10/1915
War Diary	Essars	15/10/1915	16/10/1915
War Diary	Preol	17/10/1915	20/10/1915
War Diary	Lenglet	21/10/1915	22/10/1915
War Diary	In The Train	23/10/1915	24/10/1915
War Diary	Marseilles	25/10/1915	26/10/1915
War Diary	As Shift	27/10/1915	31/10/1915
Miscellaneous	Messages And Signals.		

Miscellaneous	B.M. 644 & Operation Order No. 22.		
Operation(al) Order(s)	O.O. No. 22 By Lt. Col. W.H. Blake D.S.O. Comdg 2/East Yorkshire Regt	04/10/1915	04/10/1915

W095/22751

28TH DIVISION
83RD INFY BDE

2ND BN EAST YORKS REGT

JAN - OCT 1915

To SALONIKA

83rd Infantry Brigade.

28th Division.

Battn.
(Arrived France from
England 16.1.15).

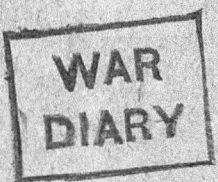

2nd BATTN. EAST YORKSHIRE REGIMENT.

J A N U A R Y

1 9 1 5

(15.1.15 to 31.1.15)

On His Majesty's Service.

Confidential

War Diary
of

2nd Batt'n. East Yorkshire Regt.

from 15.1.15 to 31.1.15

(Volume I)

WAR DIARY
or
INTELLIGENCE SUMMARY.

(Erase heading not required.)

Instructions regarding War Diaries and Intelligence Summaries are contained in F.S. Regs., Part II, and the Staff Manual respectively. Title pages will be prepared in manuscript.

Hour, Date, Place.	Summary of Events and Information.	Remarks and references to Appendices
1915 15th Jan. 8.30am Nunhead	The Battalion (Strength 26 officers 968 other ranks) marked off from billets, arrived Southampton Dock gate No 2 at 12.40 p.m. when they entrained on S.S. "City of Edinburgh".	March Table App.t I
16th Jan.	Arrived Havre docks 11.30 a.m. disembarking immediately arrived point 3 of entrainment Havre Station 5.30 p.m. Entrainment completed 9 p.m. Two platoons A Coy left behind with instructions to follow by later train. Train with H.Q. left 9.16	
17th Jan.	Arrived Rouen 1.1 a.m. Ordered from depot left Station here to join A.Q.'s department at Havre. The Battn arrived at HAZEBROUCK the point of detrainment at 5.30 p.m. were billeted in the Hospital (not yet finished being built) where the 2 Platoons A Coy. rejoined.	9/15
18 Jan. Meteren	Marched off from HAZEBROUCK at 9 a.m. and arrived at Billets 12.15 p.m. – there were provided by farm houses along a north and south line ½ mile W. of a line drawn from METEREN to OUTTERSTEENE.	
19 Jan.th 20 Jan	Route marching, entrenching and what of trenches by night practised daily	
th Jan	Orders received through 83rd Bde. that Quarter Masters and Hon Major T.J. Cunningham to report at Infantry Depot Boulogne, Sergeant ...	

WAR DIARY
or
INTELLIGENCE SUMMARY.

Army Form C. 2118.

(Erase heading not required.)

Hour, Date, Place.	Summary of Events and Information.	Remarks and references to Appendices
1915 26, 27 Jan METEREN	Route marching and chief Trenches practiced	
28th Jan "	The 83rd Brigade was inspected at 11.30 am by Field Marshal Sir John French. The Battalion paraded (20 Officers 850 other ranks under Lt Col M J Sweetman).	7/15th
29th Jan "	Entrenching practiced by Battalion in the morning.	
30th Jan "	Certain farms occupied by A Coy. were evacuated in order to make room for the City of Portsmouth Bn. which arrived in the morning. After a day of keen frost a slight thaw set in.	
31st Jan "	Orders received for all Transport except 2 Buffalo wagons to be ready to move off in evening for VLAMERTINGHE	

83rd Infantry Brigade.
28th Division.

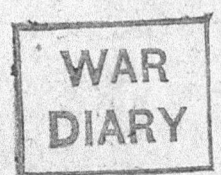

2nd BATTN. EAST YORKSHIRE REGIMENT.

F E B R U A R Y

1 9 1 5

On His Majesty's Service.

Army Form C. 2118.

WAR DIARY
or
INTELLIGENCE SUMMARY
(Erase heading not required.)

Instructions regarding War Diaries and Intelligence Summaries are contained in F. S. Regs, Part II. and the Staff Manual respectively. Title pages will be prepared in manuscript.

Hour, Date, Place	Summary of Events and Information	Remarks and references to Appendices
6 P.M. 1/2/15 VLAMERTINGHE.	Arrived by Motor Bus at 6 p.m. having left METEREN about 1 p.m. and proceeded by march route to YPRES where the Battalion was quartered at CHATEAU ROSENDAEL.	
2 a.m. 2/3/15, YPRES.	Arrived at CHATEAU ROSENDAEL where the Battalion remained in support for the day. Later in the day "C" Coy. (Capt: B.C. WILKINSON) proceeded to the CHATEAU LANGHOF and "D" Coy. (MAJOR W.N. PIKE) to the dugouts on the Canal bank. "A" and "B" Coy's. (MAJOR T.R.E.W. SWETTENHAM and CAPT. L.G. HILL respectively) remaining at CHATEAU ROSENDAEL. All Companies were shelled during the day.	
5.30 p.m. 4/4/15, YPRES.	Half "A" and "B" Coy. went into the trenches with Batt'n. Head Quarters at FERME LA CHAPELLE. At 5.30 p.m. "C" and "D" Coy. occupied trenches S. of YPRES in relief of K.O.Y.L.I. Heavy rifle fire all night and occasional shell fire. 2nd Lieut: H.J. MILLER wounded. Half "A" Coy. remained in support at CHATEAU ROSENDAEL.	
6 a.m. 4/3/15, YPRES	In the early morning the GERMANS attacked trenches to the right and left of "D" Coy. At about 6 a.m. "B" Coy. was attacked on right and driven from right portion of trench losing two Machine Guns.	

1247 W 3299 200,000 (E) 8/14 J.B.C. & A. Forms/C. 2118/11.

WAR DIARY
or
INTELLIGENCE SUMMARY

(Erase heading not required.)

Army Form C. 2118.

Hour, Date, Place	Summary of Events and Information	Remarks and references to Appendices
(Continued)	Last in the day the remainder of "B" Coy was forced to retire from the remaining portion of the trench, falling back in good order to the Grenadiers. Casualties in the early morning retirement :- Killed 6, Wounded 28, Missing 13. On the same evening an attempt was made to re-take the trench but failed owing to being unable to locate the enemy in the thick wood. In the afternoon Captain O.C. WILKINSON and Lieut: O.J. ADDYMAN were killed by the same shell. "A" and "B" Coys were relieved on the night of 11/2/15 by KINGS OWN Regiment. In the evening another attempt was made to re-take the lost trench. On arrival of the force composed of 2 Coys of E. YORK. REG. and 2 Coys of K.O.Y.L.I. under command of LIEUT. COLONEL M.J. SWEETMAN, the trench was found empty, but owing to the darkness the identity of the trench was mistaken. This resulted in the force finding itself on the GERMAN lines where they were opposed by heavy rifle fire. Casualties :- MAJOR T.R.E.W. SWEETENHAM killed	11/2
5/2/15. YPRES.		

Army Form C. 2118.

WAR DIARY
or
INTELLIGENCE SUMMARY

(Erase heading not required.)

Instructions regarding War Diaries and Intelligence Summaries are contained in F.S. Regs., Part II. and the Staff Manual respectively. Title pages will be prepared in manuscript.

Hour, Date, Place	Summary of Events and Information	Remarks and references to Appendices
(Continued)	and CAPTAIN and ADJUTANT H.F. WAILES wounded. Other ranks :- Killed 1, Wounded 8, Missing 4. Owing to a message having been received from the Brigadier (BRIG. GENERAL R.C. BOYLE, C.B.), to the effect that the force must return before daybreak, it retired, thereby losing any advantage that would otherwise have been gained.	
5.30.p.m. 8/3/15. YPRES.	The Battalion this "D" Coy., left CHATEAU ROSENDAEL at 5.30 p.m. and marched to VLAMERTINGHE, arriving at 9.30 p.m. [and were accommodated in wooden and canvas huts situated on the VLAMERTINGHE – RENNINGHELST Road.]	8/3/15
10. a.m. 9/3/15. VLAMERTINGHE.	"D" Coy. arrived about 10. a.m. This Company had been relieved in the trenches the previous night by the E. KENT REG. (THE BUFFS) and had marched to the Infantry Barracks, YPRES, where they had spent the remainder of the night of 8/3 – 9/3.	
Forenoon 8/3/15 VLAMERTINGHE	MAJOR H.H. POWELL assumed Command of the Battalion vice LIEUT. COL. M.J. SWEETMAN on the forenoon of the 8th instant, during the temporary	

WAR DIARY
or
INTELLIGENCE SUMMARY

(Erase heading not required.)

Army Form C. 2118.

Instructions regarding War Diaries and Intelligence Summaries are contained in F.S. Regs, Part II. and the Staff Manual respectively. Title pages will be prepared in manuscript.

Hour, Date, Place	Summary of Events and Information	Remarks and references to Appendices
(Continued)	absence of the latter and LIEUT. H.C.R. SAUNDERS took over the duties of Adjutant vice WAILES wounded.	
NOON 9/5/15 VLAMERTINGHE	The Battalion paraded at 10 noon when they were addressed by MAJOR GENERAL E.S. BULFIN, C.V.O., C.B. who delivered a message from the Army Commander LIEUT. GENERAL SIR H.C.O. PLUMER, K.C.B., expressing his displeasure at the unfortunate occurrence of the night of 2nd - 3rd inst. He afterwards interviewed the Officers of the Battalion. Major W.F. SWENY, THE ROYAL FUSILIERS, took over Command of the Battalion. Battalion resting.	
10/5/15 VLAMERTINGHE		10/5/15
11/5/15 YPRES.	The Battalion marched from VLAMERTINGHE to YPRES thence to TULERIE where it received ammunition, stores &c, afterwards relieving the NORTHUMBERLAND FUSILIERS in A.B.C. and D. trenches, Left Section.	

WAR DIARY
or
INTELLIGENCE SUMMARY

(Erase heading not required.)

Army Form C. 2118.

Hour, Date, Place	Summary of Events and Information	Remarks and references to Appendices
(Continued)	A quiet night. Trenches fairly good except forward portion of ZWARTELEEN - B trench - which was rather badly enfiladed. [C.O. and 2ⁿᵈ in Command (LIEUT. COLONEL W.F. SWENY and MAJOR H.H. POWELL) visited A and B. Trenches.]	
12/3/15 YPRES.	Considerable sniping. [Brigadier visit trenches in the evening and C.O. takes him to see S.1. S.2. and A.1. and A.2. trenches] Casualties: Killed 5, Wounded 12.	M.S.A.
13/3/15 YPRES.	Heavy rain.	
14/3/15 YPRES.	Battalion in support. [O.C. proceeded to Brigade Head Quarters for report and instructions.] Battalion on night relieves a similar attack Regiment – UNKNOWN. New Mather reshuffled and several (39 in all) sick with frost bite. Heavy rain.	
15/3/15 YPRES.	On night of 15ᵗʰ the Battalion goes into fire trenches relieving THE KING'S OWN. Five Casualties during night. Trenches quiet. Trenches very wet. [C.O. visits D.1., C.1., and C.2.]	

WAR DIARY
or
INTELLIGENCE SUMMARY

(Erase heading not required.)

Army Form C. 2118.

Hour, Date, Place	Summary of Events and Information	Remarks and references to Appendices
1H/2/15. YPRES.	Major H.H. POWELL visits all trenches during the night. Trenches very wet. A quiet day and night. Casualties:- Killed 2. Wounded 3.	
5.30 a.m. 17/2/15. YPRES.	ZWARTELEEN ACTION. At 5.30 a.m. the forward portion of B.2. trench was blown in and trench occupied by enemy, by a mine. Retaken at 11.30 a.m. with assistance of KING'S OWN. REG., supporting Company under MAJOR O.C. BORRETT ("A" Coy.) who made a most dashing attack- capturing 6 of the enemy and killing 25. Our casualties were very slight, considering the importance of retaking of this point, amounting to Killed 31, Wounded 33 and knowing it. Capt: L.G. HILL and Lieut: D. CAMPBELL, R.A.M.C. were included in the above number killed, and LIEUT. H.C.R SAUNDERS wounded. The enemy shelled our lines heavily all day and all our Artillery were firing over our heads too — Sometimes very short. Capt: J.B.D. TRIMBLE wounded. A quiet night. We handed over A.I. and B trenches	7/15th

Army Form C. 2118.

WAR DIARY
or
INTELLIGENCE SUMMARY
(Erase heading not required.)

Instructions regarding War Diaries and Intelligence Summaries are contained in F. S. Regs., Part II. and the Staff Manual respectively. Title pages will be prepared in manuscript.

Hour, Date, Place	Summary of Events and Information	Remarks and references to Appendices
(Continued) 17/3/15. YPRES.	To the KING'S OWN Regiment and took over support. The following telegrams were received during the evening:— No. B.M.x.14 (To. O.C. E. YORK REG) "Congratulate you on recapturing trenches" (Signd.) R.C. BOYLE, Brig: Genl. No. Nil. (To O.C. KING'S OWN and EAST.YORKSHIRE) "Message received from G.O.C. (28th 29th) Congratulations on excellent results as I always expected. BULFIN". No. B.M. 365. (To. O.C. all units 83rd BRIGADE). "Message received from Commander Fifth Corps. Very glad to hear your message B.M. 263. I am sure you and your Brigade have done very good work today" Remains in support and holding "C" and "D" trenches. During the night invaded over "C" and "D" trenches	
18/3/15 YPRES		

WAR DIARY
or
INTELLIGENCE SUMMARY

(Erase heading not required.)

Army Form C. 2118.

Instructions regarding War Diaries and Intelligence Summaries are contained in F. S. Regs., Part II. and the Staff Manual respectively. Title pages will be prepared in manuscript.

Hour, Date, Place	Summary of Events and Information	Remarks and references to Appendices
(Continued) 18/3/15. YPRES.	to K.O.Y.L.I. Held A.2 and D.2 and TUILERIE north "D" Company and HEAD QRS. at YPRES Infantry Barracks. Casualties: Killed 3. Wounded 3.	
4 p.m. 19/3/15 YPRES.	As during the night, till orders were received at 4 p.m. to take over part of S.2, #A.1 and B.1. which was done.	
20/3/15.	Battalion relieved by a Unit of XIII Brigade.	
VLAMERTINGHE 21/3/15.	Battalion in Hutments resting.	
22/3/15.	— do —	
23/3/15.	— do —	
24/3/15.	— do —	
25/3/15.	Heavy snow. Battalion resting. Visited by LIEUT. GENERAL SIR H.C.O. PLUMER, K.C.B.	
26/3/15.	Battalion resting. Heavy snow during night. Battalion left for trenches near ZILLABECK which were occupied by "B" Coy. (CAPT. B.O. TATHAM), "C" Coy. (CAPT. E.S.A. DOUGLAS) "D" Coy. and half "A" Coy. (LIEUT.	

Army Form C. 2118.

WAR DIARY
or
INTELLIGENCE SUMMARY
(Erase heading not required.)

Instructions regarding War Diaries and Intelligence Summaries are contained in F. S. Regs., Part II. and the Staff Manual respectively. Title pages will be prepared in manuscript.

Hour, Date, Place	Summary of Events and Information	Remarks and references to Appendices
(Continued)	W.W.B.BROADLEY) in the fire trenches, the remaining half Coy. of "A" in the TUILERIE. The remainder of Area "D" (Commanded by MAJOR H.H. POWELL) being held by KING'S OWN and one Company of YORK and LANCASTER Regiment. The relief was successfully carried out by 11.15 p.m.	
1.15 a.m. 27/3/15. ZILLEBEKE	At 1.15 a.m. the E.O.C. DIVISION (MAJOR GENERAL E.S. BULFIN, C.V.O., C.B.) visited the fire trenches. He came to see salient at ZWARTELIEN, that being the most dangerous point in the line. At about 3.40 p.m. the parapet of B.2. trench (4H) was blown away by enemy's trench mortar. Trench was repaired by one Platoon of "D" Coy., and parapet was repaired at once. Casualties Killed 6. Wounded 13. Other attempts were made during the afternoon to blow other portions of the trench down by trench	2/15 2/15 (?)

Army Form C. 2118.

WAR DIARY
or
INTELLIGENCE SUMMARY

(Erase heading not required.)

Instructions regarding War Diaries and Intelligence Summaries are contained in F. S. Regs., Part II. and the Staff Manual respectively. Title pages will be prepared in manuscript.

Hour, Date, Place	Summary of Events and Information	Remarks and references to Appendices
(Continued)	mortars and shell fire. 6 additional wounded during the 24 hours. Capt: and Adjt: Adjutant K.T. WOODMASS worked the trenches during the afternoon.	
28/2/15. ZILLEBEKE.	Fairly quiet day. No casualties. Total casualties to 28/2/15:- Killed 68, Wounded 132, Missing 17. includes 5 Officers killed and 5 wounded.	

83rd Infantry Brigade.

28th Division.

with Bde.
Battn. temporarily attached/ to
5th Div. from 3.3.15, rejoining
28th Div. .4.15.

WAR
DIARY

2nd BATTN. EAST YORKSHIRE REGIMENT

M A R C H

1 9 1 5

On His Majesty's Service.

Army Form C. 2118.

WAR DIARY
or
INTELLIGENCE SUMMARY
(Erase heading not required.)

Hour, Date, Place	Summary of Events and Information	Remarks and references to Appendices
1/3/15 ZILLEBEKE	Trenches heavily shelled from 10.30 A.M. to 12 noon. Trenches badly damaged by trench mortars and artillery fire. Relieved by R.W. KENT REG. and 2/- K.O.Y.L.I. Casualties:- Killed 2, wounded 1. Marched via YPRES [where the Battalion had tea] to VLAMERTINGHE.	
2 A.M. 2/3/15 (VLAMERTINGHE)	Battalion arrived from YPRES at 2 A.M. and were quartered in wooden huts [where they rested for the remainder of the night.] Capt. C.P. BERTHON and Lieut. S. HASWELL joined Battalion left VLAMERTINGHE at 8 A.M. for BAILLEUL where it arrived at 12 noon [being billeted in RUE de SUD and RUE de MOULINS with Head Qrs at RUE de GARE.]	
12 noon 3/3/15 BAILLEUL		
4/3/15 — do —	Battalion resting. Visited by Major General T.L.N MORLAND.C.B.D.S.O. Comdg. V Division.	
5/3/15 — do —	Resting in billets. Trenches about the occupied at WULVERGHEM visited by Major PIKE	

WAR DIARY
INTELLIGENCE SUMMARY
(Erase heading not required.)

Army Form C. 2118.

Hour, Date, Place	Summary of Events and Information	Remarks and references to Appendices
6/3/15. BAILLEUL	Major BERTHON, Captain TATHAM and BROADLEY and Capt OTTLEY. Machine Gun Officer. The following Officers joined the Battalion:— (5 2nd Lieuts) D.D. ANDERSON " " G.C. TATE " " N.L.C. De RINZY " " F.W.S. HUBBERT " " H.D. PAYNE Resting in billets.	
2.30 PM 7/3/15 NEUVE EGLISE	2nd Lieut. C.J.T. CAREW joined. Battalion left for trenches at WULVERGHEM near NEUVE EGLISE at 2.30 P.M. Relieved by 1/ WELCH REG. Trenches occupied as follows:— 14 B — — "A" Coy. 15 — — "C" — 14 B Support — "A" — 15 — -do- Battalion Reserve { ½ B Coy } at COOKERS FARM. { ½ D — } { ½ B — } at TEA FARM. Hd. Qrs. Casualties:- Wounded 1.	

WAR DIARY
or
INTELLIGENCE SUMMARY

Army Form C. 2118.

(Erase heading not required.)

Hour, Date, Place	Summary of Events and Information	Remarks and references to Appendices
8/3/15 WULVERGHEM	Quiet day. Lieut Col. W.F. SWENY returned from leave in England. Major POWELL visited all trenches. Casualties:- wounded 4.	
9/3/15 — do —	Quiet morning. Our artillery shelled enemy's trenches successfully. Capt R.I. RAWSON. GLOSTER REG. (Army T.F.) attached for purpose of studying mode of trench warfare for two days. 9th and 10th. "A" and "C" Coys relieved in fire trenches by "B" and "D" Coys. C.O. and Adjt. visited trenches during night. 10 casualties up to noon:- Killed 1. Wounded 3. [including Sergt JOYCE who died later in the day and was buried in DRANOUTRE Churchyard.] No. 9305 Pte W. CHEEK awarded Distinguished Conduct Medal for conspicuous bravery as stated in	

Army Form C. 2118.

WAR DIARY
INTELLIGENCE SUMMARY
(Erase heading not required.)

Instructions regarding War Diaries and Intelligence Summaries are contained in F. S. Regs., Part II. and the Staff Manual respectively. Title pages will be prepared in manuscript.

Hour, Date, Place	Summary of Events and Information	Remarks and references to Appendices
	The following Order:— "Brigade Montrose Orders by Brig General R.C. BOYLE, C.B., Commanding 83rd Brigade dd. 10/3/15. 184 Distinguished Conduct. Action for shed Commander. At ZWARTELEEN on 17th February Adviated in working Machine Gun with greatest Coolness and disregard of personal safety under heavy rifle and shell fire until his Emplacement was blown down. During the engagement a billet penetrated the water jacket and wounded Private CHEEK, but he continued to serve his gun with courage and determination during the rest of the action."	
10/3/15 WULVERGHEM	Our Artillery shelled Enemy's trenches for nearly an hour with excellent results, otherwise	

Army Form C. 2118.

WAR DIARY
INTELLIGENCE SUMMARY
(Erase heading not required.)

Instructions regarding War Diaries and Intelligence Summaries are contained in F. S. Regs., Part II. and the Staff Manual respectively. Title pages will be prepared in manuscript.

Hour, Date, Place	Summary of Events and Information	Remarks and references to Appendices
8 РM 11/3/15 WULVERGHEM	All quiet. Major POWELL visited the trenches during the night. Casualties 1 now. Wounded 3.	
12/3/15 DRANOUTRE	Quiet day. Major POWELL visited the trenches. Battalion relieved by KINGS OWN REG. about 8 PM and marched to billets at DRANOUTRE arriving about 1 AM. Casualties known :- killed 2, wounded 3, wounded 3. 2nd Lieut. H. BALL joined.	
13/3/15 — do —	Battalion in billets. Orders to be held in readiness to move during to attack on Hill 76. Battalion resting in billets.	
2 PM 14/3/15 — do —	Battalion left DRANOUTRE at 2 PM and marched to BAILLEUL (where it was billeted in RUE de FOULONS.) C.O. and Company Officers took trenches in	

1217 W 3299 200,000 (E) 8/14 J.B.C. & A. Forms/C. 2118/11.

WAR DIARY
or
INTELLIGENCE SUMMARY

(Erase heading not required.)

Army Form C. 2118.

Hour, Date, Place	Summary of Events and Information	Remarks and references to Appendices
15/3/15 BAILLEUL	PLOEGSTEERT. Battalion resting but under orders to move at short notice. Still under orders to move to unknown destination (afterwards ascertained to be PLOEGSTEERT) Cancelled at 1.30 P.M. Men allowed to quit billets as usual.	
16/3/15	2nd Lieuts. R.B. CRACROFT and W.L. HAWKINS-JONES. Resting in billets.	
1.15 PM 17/3/15 DRANOUTRE	Move at 1.15 PM to DRANOUTRE and take over 14 and 15 trenches at WULVERGHEM. Quiet night. Casualties:— Killed 2, wounded 1. Lieut. H. BALL wounded.	
18/3/15 WULVERGHEM	Dig communicating trench to 15 and more gap. Pioneers under Sergt. ROWLEY do very fine work. Patrol consisting of Sergt. PARKES and	

Army Form C. 2118.

WAR DIARY
INTELLIGENCE SUMMARY
(Erase heading not required.)

Instructions regarding War Diaries and Intelligence Summaries are contained in F. S. Regs., Part II. and the Staff Manual respectively. Title pages will be prepared in manuscript.

Hour, Date, Place	Summary of Events and Information	Remarks and references to Appendices
3 PM 19/3/15. WULVERGHEM	Private OTTEWELL & section whilst mine was being laid went to enemys trenches and to avenge death of two men, killed earlier in the day, threw hand grenades into them. Casualties:- wounded 5. including Lieut G.C.TATE. Heavy guns in morning - very quiet day. Artillery fire a little at 3 PM. Fri trenches relieved by other Companies. Casualties:- wounded 2, including Lieut W.E.F. DAVIDSON.	
20/3/15	Slight frost in morning - Quiet day. Lieut H.D. PAYNE hit in pelvis and died at Battalion Head Qrs. (TEA FARM). [Buried in DRANOUTRE Churchyard at 9.30 PM] Casualties:- wounded 3. Lieut G.C.TATE dies of his wounds [came in BAILLEUL.]	

WAR DIARY
INTELLIGENCE SUMMARY
(Erase heading not required.)

Army Form C. 2118.

Hour, Date, Place	Summary of Events and Information	Remarks and references to Appendices
21/3/15 WULVERGHEM	Battalion Head Qrs. Changed from TEA FARM to ELBOW FARM and take over 10A and 11B trenches. At once commence work on parapets. Casualties :- wounded 2.	
22/3/15 -do-	Quiet day. Two snipers silenced and dealt with. Casualties:- wounded 4.	
23/3/15 -do-	Enemy shelled 10A trench and NEUVE EGLISE. 6 men and one Civilian wounded and two horses killed at latter place while transporting the Quartermaster's Stores from the Convent to the BULFORD CAMP huttments which had been allotted to the Battalion on being relieved in the trenches. Casualties including above :- killed 3, wounded 11. Relieved by 5t. Kings Own Regt. about 10 PM and proceeded to NEUVE EGLISE.	

WAR DIARY or INTELLIGENCE SUMMARY

Army Form C. 2118.

Hour, Date, Place	Summary of Events and Information	Remarks and references to Appendices
24/3/15 NEUVE EGLISE	Battalion resting - 250 Men detailed for digging trenches.	
25/3/15 do	Battalion resting. Brigadier sees all Officers re System of work in the trenches.	
26/3/15 do	Commences instruction in trench action on Captains of Henny's trenches - 250 men dig near outer line of trenches under R.E. supervision. Casualties :- wounded 1.	
27/3/15 do	New double skins loop holes inspected by Battalion Officers. One telescopic rifle - introduced for use against Henny's Snipers received - Rifle found to be inaccurately sighted.	
28/3/15 do	Church Parade at ALDERSHOT CAMP huttments.	

WAR DIARY
INTELLIGENCE SUMMARY
(Erase heading not required.)

Army Form C. 2118.

Hour, Date, Place	Summary of Events and Information	Remarks and references to Appendices
29/3/15 WULVERGHEM	Battalion proceeded to WULVERGHEM and occupied 10.A, 10.B, and 11.A. trenches and support Point 5. Supporting Companies occupy BUS FARM, BURNT FARM and DRESSING STATION and Head Qrs at GABLE FARM. Enemy fires on working party in front of 10 A which has to cease work. No Casualties.	
30/3/15	Fine. Cold and frosty. Quiet day. Enemy still sniping from the left. Enemy shelled WULVERGHEM. Head Qrs party dig dug-outs. Trenches enlarged & flanks. Traverses and parados constructed and improved. Casualties:- wounded 4.	

Army Form C. 2118.

WAR DIARY
INTELLIGENCE SUMMARY
(Erase heading not required.)

Hour, Date, Place	Summary of Events and Information	Remarks and references to Appendices
31/3/15 WULVERGHEM	Officer patrol under Lieut G.R.P. WOOKEY report enemy very busy on wire and attending trench in front of 10.A - Flares were placed between 10.A and 10.B. Communicating trench from 10.B. inspected by 2.O and 2nd in Command who decide to clean and improve it - working party works at night. Ten rounds rapid fire at enemy working party at much cipher them to cease work. Nobody actually wounded. Casualties:- Casualties { Officers — Killed Nil, Wounded 1 (2 died) for Month { O.Ranks — Killed 11, Wounded 48, Missing Nil (2 died) Casualties { 7 8 up to and for { 81 173 16 31/3/15	It is Sunny Lord Clive. Komds: After Wiltshire Regt.

Forms/C. 2118/11.

12/5405.

83/
28th Division.

2nd East Yorkshire Reg.

Vol IV   1 – 30.4.15

G.F.
15 sheets

Army Form C. 2118.

WAR DIARY
or
INTELLIGENCE SUMMARY

(Erase heading not required.)

Instructions regarding War Diaries and Intelligence Summaries are contained in F. S. Regs., Part II. and the Staff Manual respectively. Title pages will be prepared in manuscript.

Hour, Date, Place	Summary of Events and Information	Remarks and references to Appendices
1/4/15 WULVERGHEM	Quiet day. Enemy shelled 10 B & 11 A. A. Redoubt. Major Powell finished digging Communicating Trench to 10 B. Hand over 11 A & S.P. 5 to 5/ N. STAFFORD Regt. Take over 1 A & 15. S. from YORK & LANC. Regt. Casualties :- Killed 1. Wounded 1.	
2/4/15 — do —	Dull day. Very quiet. Enemy fire at our Aeroplanes which reveals that they are holding trenches pretty strongly. Hand over 10 A & 10 B to SOUTH STAFFORD Regt. 1 A to 84½ Brigade. Casualties :- Wounded 2. Sergt. Parkes (included among the wounded) has done excellent work during the last month & has been recommended for recognition. During the tour Cadets of the BAILEUL Training School constantly visited the trenches, mostly members of the H.A.C. & ARTIST RIFLES. Left for BAILEUL the same night.	

Army Form C. 2118.

WAR DIARY
or
INTELLIGENCE SUMMARY
(Erase heading not required.)

Instructions regarding War Diaries and Intelligence Summaries are contained in F. S. Regs, Part II. and the Staff Manual respectively. Title pages will be prepared in manuscript.

Hour, Date, Place	Summary of Events and Information	Remarks and references to Appendices
2.30 p.m. 3/4/15 BAILLEUL	Left for WESTOUTRE at 2.30 p.m. Lieut. Z.A. TURTON joined.	
4/4/15 WESTOUTRE	Battalion Resting.	
5/4/15 —do—	Lieut: G.H. VASEY joined. Battalion Resting.	
6/4/15 —do—	Company Commanders inspect new trenches at ZONNEBEKE. 2nd Lieut: S.E. CALLARD & draft of 39 joined.	
7/4/15 —do—	Battalion inspected by GEN. SIR H.L. SMITH-DORRIEN. G.C.B., D.S.O.	
5 p.m. 8/4/15 —do—	Battalion left for YPRES by Motor Buss at 5 p.m. Transport proceeded by road.	
8 p.m. 9/4/15 YPRES	Battalion arrived at 6 p.m. & after receiving a second days rations proceeded by Companies at intervals of 20 minutes commencing at 8 p.m. to ZONNEBEKE. Trenches previously occupied by 146th French Regt. found to be in very bad condition, undrained & communicating trenches too shallow, insufficiently traversed & parapet often not bullet proof. Casualties :- Killed 5. Wounded 7.	
10/4/15 ZONNEBEKE	Quiet day. Casualties :- Killed 2. Wounded 3.	

WAR DIARY
or
INTELLIGENCE SUMMARY

(Erase heading not required.)

Army Form C. 2118.

Hour, Date, Place	Summary of Events and Information	Remarks and references to Appendices
11/4/15. ZONNEBEKE	Quiet day. Two bombs dropped by Taube near Battalion Hd. Quarters in POLYGON WOOD. No damage done as bombs did not explode. Casualties :- Killed 2. Wounded 2. Draft of 66 joined.	
10p.m 12/4/15 -do-	Battalion relieved by 1/K.O.Y.L.I. at 10p.m. & proceeded to YPRES where the Battalion was quartered in the LUNATIC ASYLUM, N.E. of town.	
13/4/15. YPRES.	Resting in billets.	
14/4/15 -do-	Resting in billets. 2nd Lieuts. D.H. LAYTON & R.F. SIMNETT joined.	
15/4/15 ZONNEBEKE	Battalion proceeded to ZONNEBEKE & occupied trenches A, B, & C. in relief of 1/K.O.Y.L.I. These trenches were afterwards numbered 1, 2, & 3. The trenches were occupied as follows :- "A" Coy. No. 1. "D" Coy. No. 2. & "C" Coy. No. 3 with "B" Coy. in support on Hd. 8th in POLYGON WOOD. Trenches in very bad condition, particularly No. 2.	

Army Form C. 2118.

WAR DIARY
or
INTELLIGENCE SUMMARY

(Erase heading not required.)

Instructions regarding War Diaries and Intelligence Summaries are contained in F. S. Regs., Part II. and the Staff Manual respectively. Title pages will be prepared in manuscript.

Hour, Date, Place	Summary of Events and Information	Remarks and references to Appendices
16/4/15 ZONNEBEKE	Quiet day. Casualties: Killed 2. Wounded 5. 2/Lieut: C.H. ARMITAGE joined.	
17/4/15 —do—	Quiet day. Received & tested new Trench Mortar (Improved 3.7 Trench Mortar). This one was found to be a great improvement on those previously in use & a report to that effect was sent to 83rd Brigade. Casualties:- Wounded 2.	
18/4/15 —do—	Enemy use Trench Mortars against us. Casualties:- Wounded 13.	
19/4/15 —do—	Town of YPRES violently bombarded all day & night. Quiet day. Relieved by 1/K.O.Y.L.I. at 10 p.m. & proceeded to "A" Huttments arriving at 3 a.m. 20/4/15. Casualties:- Killed 3. Wounded 1.	
20/4/15 YPRES.	Resting in huttments.	
21/4/15 —do—	Resting in huttments. 2/Lieut: R.C. FISH & draft of 114 joined.	Les be 21st K.15. W 38

Army Form C. 2118.

WAR DIARY
or
INTELLIGENCE SUMMARY
(Erase heading not required.)

Hour, Date, Place	Summary of Events and Information	Remarks and references to Appendices
6.30 p.m. 22/4/15. YPRES.	Battalion ordered to "Stand to" at 6.30 p.m. in consequence of the Germans having broken through the line held by the FRENCH Army near ST. JULIEN. Marched to BRIELEN & bivouacked in field during the night.	
4.30 p.m. 23/4/15 ST. JEAN.	The Battalion together with YORK & LANC. Regt. & ST. MONMOUTH Regt. were formed into a Composite Brigade under the Command of LIEUT. COLONEL A.D. GEDDES, Commanding "THE BUFFS" & sent to the CANADIAN DIVISION which was Commanded by LIEUT. GENERAL E.A.H. ALDERSON, C.B. The Battalion first moved into trenches in MOUSE T. of ST. JEAN. At 4.30 p.m. an order was received to advance & attack the GERMAN position some 1500 yards to our front. The attack was carried out with great energy & dash but owing to the heavy shell fire & the number of Machine	

Instructions regarding War Diaries and Intelligence Summaries are contained in F. S. Regs., Part II. and the Staff Manual respectively. Title pages will be prepared in manuscript.

WAR DIARY
or
INTELLIGENCE SUMMARY
(Erase heading not required.)

Army Form C. 2118.

Instructions regarding War Diaries and Intelligence Summaries are contained in F. S. Regs, Part II. and the Staff Manual respectively. Title pages will be prepared in manuscript.

Hour, Date, Place	Summary of Events and Information	Remarks and references to Appendices
4.30 a.m. 5.30 p.m.	Guns employed against us the Battalion suffered such heavy losses that when about 100 yards from the enemy's trenches (portions of our line had advanced to within 30 yds.) it was found that, even if the Battalion had succeeded in reaching the enemy's trenches - which is doubtful - it would have been unable to hold them, so orders were given for them to retire.	
5.30 p.m.	Greatest courage was displayed throughout by all ranks. The spirit & tenacity of the men is shown by the fact that a party of men, under Corporal HALL, who for some unaccountable reason did not receive the order to retire, actually entrenched themselves within 30 yards of the enemy, where they remained undisturbed by the GERMANS for over 48 hours without food or water. Finding themselves isolated & not receiving orders they retired after dusk on the 25th. This incident also shows that the offensive spirit of	

WAR DIARY
or
INTELLIGENCE SUMMARY

(Erase heading not required.)

Army Form C. 2118.

Hour, Date, Place	Summary of Events and Information	Remarks and references to Appendices

The Germans was for the time broken.

This attack had checked the GERMAN advance and probably prevented the town of YPRES from falling into the hands of the enemy as it enabled reinforcements to be pushed up.

From dusk to dawn (24/4/15) the survivors with employed in carrying the wounded to the various dressing stations.

Casualties :- Officer   Other ranks
    Killed. Wounded. Missing   Killed. Wounded. Missing.
      4   9   1   41   256   42

Lieut: TURTON, who is missing was wounded when last seen & it is feared that the majority of the 42 other ranks now also killed.

The following is a list of Officers killed, wounded & missing :-

WAR DIARY
or
INTELLIGENCE SUMMARY

(Erase heading not required.)

Army Form C. 2118.

Hour, Date, Place	Summary of Events and Information	Remarks and references to Appendices

24/4/15 ST. JEAN.	Killed.- CAPT. K.T. WOODMASS.
	    -"- B.O. TATHAM.
	    2/LIEUT. F.W.S. HUBBERT.
	    -"- S. HASWELL.
	Wounded.- LIEUT. COL. W.F. SWENY (ROYAL FUS)
	    MAJOR C.P. BERTHON
	    LIEUT. D.L. HAWKINS
	    -"- S.E. CALLARD
	    -"- N.T.C. de RINZY
	    -"- R.B. CRACROFT.
	    -"- C.W. ARMITAGE
	    -"- D.H. LAYTON.
	    -"- C.J.T. CAREW.
	Missing.- LIEUT. Z.A. TURTON (of NORFOLK REG.)
	The Battalion, now about 4 Officers & 250 other ranks, re-organized in the Reserve Trenches at ST. JEAN Major H.H. POWELL in Command.	

WAR DIARY
or
INTELLIGENCE SUMMARY
(Erase heading not required.)

Army Form C. 2118.

Hour, Date, Place	Summary of Events and Information	Remarks and references to Appendices
24/4/15 ST. JEAN.	Casualties :- Killed 1. Wounded 7. Lieut. G.R.P. WOOKEY appointed Adjutant vice CAPT. K.T. WOODMASS killed.	
25/4/15 — do —	Enemy severely bombarded our trenches & the village of ST JEAN, some 300 yards behind us, happily without doing much damage. Casualties :- Killed 3. Wounded 1 Draft of 50 joined	
26/4/15 — do —	Remained in reserve trenches. While in these trenches an Indian Brigade passed through them & attacked the GERMAN position. About 7 p.m. the Battalion moved to Divisional Reserve Trenches further EAST near WIELTJE village. Casualties :- Killed 1 Wounded 1.	

WAR DIARY
or
INTELLIGENCE SUMMARY
(Erase heading not required.)

Army Form C. 2118.

Hour, Date, Place	Summary of Events and Information	Remarks and references to Appendices
	Following telegram received during day:—	
	No. B.M.104. DATED 26.4.15.	
	To ALL UNITS 28 DIVISION.	
	Following message received. Begins.— The Commander-in-Chief wishes to express to all ranks of the 28th Division his appreciation for the manner in which the 28th Division has borne itself under the strain of the last few days. A.A.A. He feels confident that they will stubbornly hold their ground for the short time that the call is made on them and add fresh laurels to their Regimental Records. A.A.A. The Corps Commander desires to endorse the Commendation of the Commander-in-Chief. A.A.A. Major General BULFIN congratulates the 28th Division on the well merited praise they have won. A.A.A. To be communicated	

Army Form C. 2118.

WAR DIARY
or
INTELLIGENCE SUMMARY
(Erase heading not required.)

Instructions regarding War Diaries and Intelligence Summaries are contained in F. S. Regs., Part II. and the Staff Manual respectively. Title pages will be prepared in manuscript.

Hour, Date, Place	Summary of Events and Information	Remarks and references to Appendices
27.4.15 ST. JEAN	To all ranks snd. FROM 83rd BRIGADE	
10.5 p.m.	Battalion heavily shelled throughout the day by high explosive & shrapnel from various points of the salient. Casualties :- Killed 1.	
11 a.m. 28.4.15 —do—	Battalion relieved at 11 a.m. & proceeded to "H" Huttments, N.W. of YPRES. On the way from the trenches the Battalion came under heavy shell fire, particularly in crossing the YSER Canal, N of YPRES, fortunately without doing much damage. Casualties:- Wounded 4. Missing 1. Following Telegram received during day :- TO ALL UNITS No. B.M.L. 71 DATED 28.4.15.	

Army Form C. 2118.

WAR DIARY
or
INTELLIGENCE SUMMARY
(Erase heading not required.)

Instructions regarding War Diaries and Intelligence Summaries are contained in F. S. Regs., Part II. and the Staff Manual respectively. Title pages will be prepared in manuscript.

Hour, Date, Place	Summary of Events and Information	Remarks and references to Appendices
29. 4. 15. YPRES.	The G.O.C. 28th Division wishes it to be made known to all ranks that their efforts whether fighting on the Northern front or doing double tour of duty in our original trenches are fully appreciated by those in Command. The Army & Corps Commanders consider that the conduct of the troops of the 28th Division has been beyond praise. (Sd) J.E. MUNBY. CAPT. B.M. 83rd BRIGADE.	
30. 4. 15. —do—	Battalion resting in hutments. 2/Lieut. E.S. SMITH and W.H. GREET joined. "C" and "D" Hutments (300 x N of "A" & "B") shelled by enemy. Draft of 63 joined – following Officers also joined :–	

WAR DIARY
or
INTELLIGENCE SUMMARY
(Erase heading not required.)

Army Form C. 2118.

Hour, Date, Place	Summary of Events and Information	Remarks and references to Appendices

	CAPT. R.S. HOPKINS. CAPT. F.S. SASSE
	LIEUT. F.G. PRICHARD. 2/LIEUT. S.H. GINN
	-//- A.F. CEMERY -//- J. KYLE
	-//- F.W.C. HININGS -//- G.A. STEVENSON
	-//- R. CRYSTAL -//- T.F. SMITH
	
	Casualties for April 1915.
	   Officers Other ranks
	Killed. Wounded. Missing Killed. Wounded. Missing
	  4 9 1 62 307 74
	
	Casualties up 15th & for 20th April 1915.
	   Officers Other ranks
	Killed Wounded Missing Killed Wounded Missing
	 11 17 1 143 480 90.
		W. Young
		Lt Colonel.
		Comdg W. Works Regt
		22/5/15.

83/28

121/5775

28th 15 Division

2nd East Yorkshire

Vol V 1 — 31.5.15.

The O/C
A.S.C.
3rd Echelon.

Herewith, original sheets of War Diary from the 26th April 1915 to 30th May 1915, inclusive of the Company under my Command, please.

In the Field.
24-6-15.

M.M.____ Lieut.

2nd Batt. East Yorkshire Regt.

WAR DIARY
or
INTELLIGENCE SUMMARY
(Erase heading not required.)

Army Form C. 2118.

Hour, Date, Place	Summary of Events and Information	Remarks and references to Appendices
YPRES 1/5/15	Battalion resting in "A" hutments.	
—do— 2/5/15	Battalion ordered at 6 p.m. to go to new trenches near FREZENBERG. Worked all night to improve them. Casualties :- Wounded 2. Message received from Lieut. Col. W. F. SWENY, Royal Fusiliers who commanded the Battalion & was wounded on 23/4/15 & read to Battalion on parade :- "Please tell the Regiment how proud I am of the gallant way they struggled on in our attack. Tell them how much I think of their splendid advance & how sorry I am that we	

Army Form C. 2118.

WAR DIARY
or
INTELLIGENCE SUMMARY
(Erase heading not required.)

Instructions regarding War Diaries and Intelligence Summaries are contained in F.S. Regs., Part II. and the Staff Manual respectively. Title pages will be prepared in manuscript.

Hour, Date, Place	Summary of Events and Information	Remarks and references to Appendices
YPRES. 3/5/15.	Could not get in of what we had such heavy losses. Battalion remained in POLYGON WOOD in reserve. Withdrawn to VELORAN HOEK. Marched up to support HAMPSHIRE REG (11th Brigade) Returned at 11 p.m. D and B Coys occupied trenches & A and C Coys to HEAD QRS.	
—do— 4/5/15.	Battalion shelled heavily from dawn to dusk. Trenches in very bad condition - full of water. Two feet wide - no dugouts & no communicating trenches. Casualties :- Capt. R. WALLACE wounded & Killed 1 & Wounded 1	
—do— 5/5/15.	Battalion violently shelled from 5 a.m. to noon and 2 to 5 p.m. GERMANS advanced up to 100 yards on night. Rest of GERMAN attack approached from 3000 to 600 yards. Part of their force was entrenched	

Army Form C. 2118.

WAR DIARY
or
INTELLIGENCE SUMMARY
(Erase heading not required.)

Instructions regarding War Diaries and Intelligence Summaries are contained in F. S. Regs., Part II. and the Staff Manual respectively. Title pages will be prepared in manuscript.

Hour, Date, Place	Summary of Events and Information	Remarks and references to Appendices

YPRES 6/5/15.	within 300 yards.
	
	Casualties:-
	
	            Missing Killed Wounded Missing
	Officers
	Killed Wounded. 10 Nil 35 134 6
	Nil. Capt: F. H. SASSE
	    -"- G. S. A. DOUGLAS.
	    -"- A. E. OTTLEY
	    -"- W. W. B. BROADLEY
	  Lieut: F. E. PRICHARD
	    -"- R. F. SIMMETT
	    -"- T. F. SMITH
	    -"- A. F. CEMERY
	    -"- S. W. FINN
	    -"- G. A. STEVENSON
	
	Relieved by 1st MONMOUTH REG and proceeded to G. H. Q. lines at POTIZJE. Slight shelling of our trenches. Heavy shelling of our guns 200 yds in rear.	

Army Form C. 2118.

WAR DIARY
or
INTELLIGENCE SUMMARY
(Erase heading not required.)

Hour, Date, Place	Summary of Events and Information	Remarks and references to Appendices

YPRES. 4/5/15.

Casualties:-

Officers.
Killed. Wounded. Missing.
Nil. 2/Lt: J. KYLE. Nil.
 " F.W.G. HININGS.

Other ranks.
Killed. Wounded. Missing.
Nil. 9. Nil.

Battalion held in continual state of readiness.
In the evening the Battalion was sent up to dig
Support trenches behind the FREZENBERG line.
Completed the work at 3 a.m. 5/5/15.

—do— 5/5/15

Casualties:-

Officers.
Killed. Wounded. Missing.
Nil. 2/Lt: R.C. FISH. Nil.

Other ranks.
Killed. Wounded. Missing.
4 8 6

At 10 a.m Battalion received orders to go up and
support 2/. MONMOUTH REG. who had been driven out
of the trenches.

Numbers actually present:- 7 Officers + 221 Other ranks.

Army Form C. 2118.

WAR DIARY
or
INTELLIGENCE SUMMARY

(Erase heading not required.)

Instructions regarding War Diaries and Intelligence Summaries are contained in F. S. Regs, Part II. and the Staff Manual respectively. Title pages will be prepared in manuscript.

Hour, Date, Place	Summary of Events and Information	Remarks and references to Appendices
	Met severe opposition at 1000 yds. Ordered to retire to G.H.Q. lines & to hold on at all costs. At 11.30 a.m. orders were received to again advance in support of 2/. MONMOUTH REG. Advance again held up. Enemy seen to be advancing in force. 300 yards. Trenches held by KINGS OWN captured by GERMANS on our left front. Retired to G.H.Q. line at 3 p.m. Received orders to re-take original line of trenches at FREZENBERG. Held up by GERMANS 1000 yards away. Held on to the ground all day & entrenched by night. Supported by one Company of E. SURREY REG. Received orders at 5 p.m. to retake original line covered by an attack to be made to our left by ROYAL WARWICK REG. and ROYAL MUNSTER FUSILIERS at 7.30 p.m. Nothing happened.	

WAR DIARY
or
INTELLIGENCE SUMMARY
(Erase heading not required.)

Army Form C. 2118.

Hour, Date, Place	Summary of Events and Information	Remarks and references to Appendices

Casualties:

	Officers			Other Ranks		
	Killed	Wounded	Missing	Killed	Wounded	Missing
	Nil	MAJOR H.H. POWELL	Nil	2	23	9
		" K.N. PIKE				
		Lieut G.R.P. WOOKEY (& missing)				
		" H. HOOPER. R.A.M.C.				

At 10 p.m. Capt: R.S. HOPKINS who had assumed Command in the forenoon, vice MAJOR W.N. PIKE, wounded, went in search of Commanding Officer of above-mentioned Regiment which had been held up by the GERMANS in trenches about ¼ mile to our immediate left. Discuss situation. O.C. ROYAL WARWICK REG went to Consult Brigadier re attack.

Ordered that attack must be carried out at 10.15 a.m. 9/5/15. Arranged all Regiments to form up opposite "Nursery trench" 300 yards to our front & on road at

Army Form C. 2118.

WAR DIARY
or
INTELLIGENCE SUMMARY
(Erase heading not required.)

Instructions regarding War Diaries and Intelligence Summaries are contained in F. S. Regs., Part II. and the Staff Manual respectively. Title pages will be prepared in manuscript.

Hour, Date, Place	Summary of Events and Information	Remarks and references to Appendices
12.45 a.m.	Advanced following order:- 2/. E. YORK. REG. 2/. KING'S OWN. E. SURREY. REG. (in support) On approaching hedgerows subjected to heavy fire by GERMANS entrenched in front of us. Unable to advance. Fell back 1', starting point, and proceeded to improve dugouts. Battalion moved 100 yards to right & proceeded to improve existing line of trenches. 2/ Lieut. D.D. ANDERSON appointed Act'g Adjutant vice LIEUT. E.R.T. WOOKEY assumed of missing.	

Army Form C. 2118.

WAR DIARY
or
INTELLIGENCE SUMMARY
(Erase heading not required.)

Instructions regarding War Diaries and Intelligence Summaries are contained in F. S. Regs., Part II. and the Staff Manual respectively. Title pages will be prepared in manuscript.

Hour, Date, Place	Summary of Events and Information	Remarks and references to Appendices

YPRES. 9/5/15.	Heavily shelled all day. Impossible to get up roads. No communication trenches. Telephone cut. Impossible to get wounded away. Casualties:-
	
	      Officer Other ranks
	 Killed Wounded Missing Killed Wounded Missing
	  Nil Nil Nil 4 4 4	

-do- 10/5/15.	Quiet morning & afternoon. Heavy shelling in the evening. Heavy & accurate rifle fire during the night. Cavalry Brigade rushed up in support. 1st Dragoon Guards on our left. MIDDLESEX REG. on our right.	
-do- 11/5/15	Relieved at 11 p.m. by THE BUFFS. Battalion headqrs "A" HUTS at 3 a.m. 11/5/15. Remainder of Brigade formed into Composite Battn	

Army Form C. 2118.

WAR DIARY
or
INTELLIGENCE SUMMARY

(Erase heading not required.)

Instructions regarding War Diaries and Intelligence Summaries are contained in F. S. Regs., Part II. and the Staff Manual respectively. Title pages will be prepared in manuscript.

Hour, Date, Place	Summary of Events and Information	Remarks and references to Appendices
YPRES. 11/5/15	and moved up to POTIJZE in support. Draft of 36 joined.	
POPERINGHE 12/5/15	Moved at 9.30 p.m. to billets at BRAND-HOEK arriving about 8 a.m. (12/5/15). Part of Batt. which had been taken to form Brigade Composite Batt. reached billets about 4 a.m. 13/5/15. Casualties:- Wounded 1. Moved to billets [at the AERODROME] N.W. of POPERINGHE which had been abandoned by ROYAL FLYING CORPS some 10 days previously & again by 18th Brigade Transport four days previously owing to its being heavily shelled by GERMAN 17 inch Howitzers. Draft of 406 men arrived (including 353 Volunteers from North Staffordshire Regt). Resting - Billets.	
—do— 13/5/15		

Army Form C. 2118.

WAR DIARY
or
INTELLIGENCE SUMMARY
(Erase heading not required.)

Instructions regarding War Diaries and Intelligence Summaries are contained in F. S. Regs, Part II. and the Staff Manual respectively. Title pages will be prepared in manuscript.

Hour, Date, Place	Summary of Events and Information	Remarks and references to Appendices
POPERINGHE 14/5/15	Moved at 7 a.m. & left by Motor Bus for WINNEZEELE for rest. reaching there at 1 p.m. Immediately commenced with reorganising & building a Battalion.	
WINNEZEELE 15/5/15	Outbreak of Scarlet fever in "B" Coy. LIEUT COLONEL W. H. YOUNG on arrival from 1st Batt. assumed Command. Following Officers also joined & posted to Companies as under :— 1 CAPT. J.C. LAMPREY "D" Coy. 4 2/LIEUT. E.S. RERRIE "A" -"- -"- R. CHRYSTAL "B" -"- -"- C.E.H. RICKETT "C" -"- -"- N.E. TRIER. "C" -"- Resting in billets.	
-do- 16.5.15		

Army Form C. 2118.

WAR DIARY
or
INTELLIGENCE SUMMARY

(Erase heading not required.)

Instructions regarding War Diaries and Intelligence Summaries are contained in F. S. Regs., Part II. and the Staff Manual respectively. Title pages will be prepared in manuscript.

Hour, Date, Place	Summary of Events and Information	Remarks and references to Appendices
WINNEZEELE 17/5/15.	Battalion inspected by LIEUT. COL. T. O. MARDEN, THE WELSH REG. Comdg 83rd Brigade. He expressed himself pleased with the general turn out of the Batt. and especially with the quick way in which the Batt. had been re-equipped — it having lost practically everything some six days previously. The Batt. which numbered 5 Officers and 883 other ranks on the 11/5/15 was paraded 14 Officers & 807 other ranks. 2nd Lieut L. B. FRERE, D.L.I. & G. B. WHITE joined.	
18/5/15	Resting in billets	
19/5/15	— do —	
20/5/15	— do — Following Officers joined & posted to Co'ys as under :— 2nd Lieut: L. L. BENKE YORKSHIRE REG. } "A" Co'y. H. W. WILSON YORKSHIRE REG.	

— 1 —

Army Form C. 2118.

WAR DIARY
or
INTELLIGENCE SUMMARY
(Erase heading not required.)

Instructions regarding War Diaries and Intelligence Summaries are contained in F. S. Regs., Part II. and the Staff Manual respectively. Title pages will be prepared in manuscript.

Hour, Date, Place	Summary of Events and Information	Remarks and references to Appendices

WINNEZEELE 21/5/15.	2/Lieut: J.A.P. WILD "B" Coy.
	— 4 — W.T. WHITE YORKSHIRE REG.
	— " — T.L. BARKAS. "C" Coy.
	  D.L.I.
	— " — H.A. WILKINSON "D" Coy.
	  YORKSHIRE REG.
	
	The Commander-in-Chief, FIELD MARSHAL SIR J.D.P. FRENCH, G.C.B, G.C.V.O, K.C.M.G. inspected the BRIGADE. He said that he wished to express his personal thanks & deep appreciation to every Officer, N.C.O. & man for their splendid work, their magnificent fighting qualities & bravery in the recent severe fighting around the YPRES salient. (SECOND BATTLE OF YPRES.)
	
	Though their past records were splendid they had never excelled the truly wonderful spirit they had manifested in the heavy fighting in question.	

Army Form C. 2118.

WAR DIARY
or
INTELLIGENCE SUMMARY
(Erase heading not required.)

Instructions regarding War Diaries and Intelligence Summaries are contained in F. S. Regs., Part II. and the Staff Manual respectively. Title pages will be prepared in manuscript.

Hour, Date, Place	Summary of Events and Information	Remarks and references to Appendices
YPRES 22/7/15	In the afternoon the Battn. proceeded to VLAMERTINGHE and bivouaced in wood N of town. Lieut: T.R. GRYLLS, LEICESTER REG. joined.	
1·30 a.m.	Relieved ½ D.C.L.I. in trenches. Relief completed at 1·30 a.m. Night moderately quiet. Machine Gun detailed to be on Hill 60 makes exceptionally good practice round Battalion Head Qrs. Capt: Hopkins visited all the trenches. Casualties :- Killed 1. Wounded 2.	
" 23/7/15	G.O. visited trenches between 10 a.m. & 12 noon. Ventilation requires attention. Work proceed during day on communication & repair of No 1 trench. G.O. visited trenches 10.30 p.m to 1 a.m. (24/7/15) Work on trenches & protection for Dugout. Casualties :- Killed 2. Wounded 1. Lieut: V. BUXTON, LEICESTER REG. joined.	

Army Form C. 2118.

WAR DIARY
or
INTELLIGENCE SUMMARY
(Erase heading not required.)

Instructions regarding War Diaries and Intelligence Summaries are contained in F. S. Regs., Part II. and the Staff Manual respectively. Title pages will be prepared in manuscript.

Hour, Date, Place	Summary of Events and Information	Remarks and references to Appendices
YPRES. 24/5/15.	Intense German shell fire commenced 3.45 a.m. & continued till 4.45 a.m. & with scarcely less intensity to 1 p.m. Report that line was broken on MENIN Road. Made ready for possible consequences. Shell fire continued again in the afternoon. 84th Brigade counter attack. C.O. visited trenches several times. Telephone Communication continually cut. Night fairly quiet & work continued on trenches. Casualties :- 2/Lieut. J.A.P. WILD wounded. Other ranks. Wounded 5. Missing 2.	
— do — 25/5/15.	Quiet day. Machine Gun still very objectionable. C.O. visited all trenches in the morning & again at night. Walls suddenly discovered in H. 4 Trench & steps taken to improve it. Work by day making latrines & filling sandbags & by Night making drains & communicating trenches. No Casualties.	

WAR DIARY or INTELLIGENCE SUMMARY

Army Form C. 2118.

Hour, Date, Place	Summary of Events and Information	Remarks and references to Appendices
YPRES 26/5/15	Quiet day except for Machine Gun. Hostile Aeroplanes very active. [C.O. & Officers YORK AND LANC REG arrive to see Trenches at 2.30 p.m.] Relieved by YORK AND LANC. REG at 10 p.m. Relief completed by 12-30 a.m (27/5/15) without casualties & proceed to SANCTUARY WOOD.	
-do- 27/5/15	Work on support trenches. Casualties :- Killed 1.	
-do- 28/5/15	-do- [C. O. & Officers of "A" and "D" Coys reconnoitre left sector at night. A patrol was	
-do- 29/5/15	-do- sent out to capture a suspected sniper with no result (?) German Guns very active at night. 2/Lieut: A. CRICK: LEIC. REG. & draft of 60 arrived.	
-do- 30/5/15	Work in morning. Relieved 1/ YORK AND LANC. REG in trenches around Communication Trench 5.0. at night leaving a garrison of 20 in a supporting work (B) in SANCTUARY WOOD. Casualties :- Wounded 3. 2/Lieut: H.E. DICKENS joined	

Army Form C. 2118.

WAR DIARY
or
INTELLIGENCE SUMMARY

(Erase heading not required.)

Hour, Date, Place	Summary of Events and Information	Remarks and references to Appendices

YPRES 31/5/15.	Quiet day. 2 Officers of INDIAN CAVALRY up to see trenches & spend night. 19.B visits trenches several times. Considerable work done on trenches. Lieut. D.A. COX, 2/Lieut. A.M. MIEVILLE & F.A. JENKINS joined.
	
	Casualties for May 1915 :-
	      Other ranks
	Officer Killed Wounded Missing Killed Wounded Missing
	Killed Wounded Missing
	Nil. 21 Nil. 46 195 37.
	
	Casualties reported up to & for 31st May 1915. :-
	            Other ranks
	Officer Killed Wounded Missing
	Killed Wounded Missing
	11 38 1 189 673 117.	

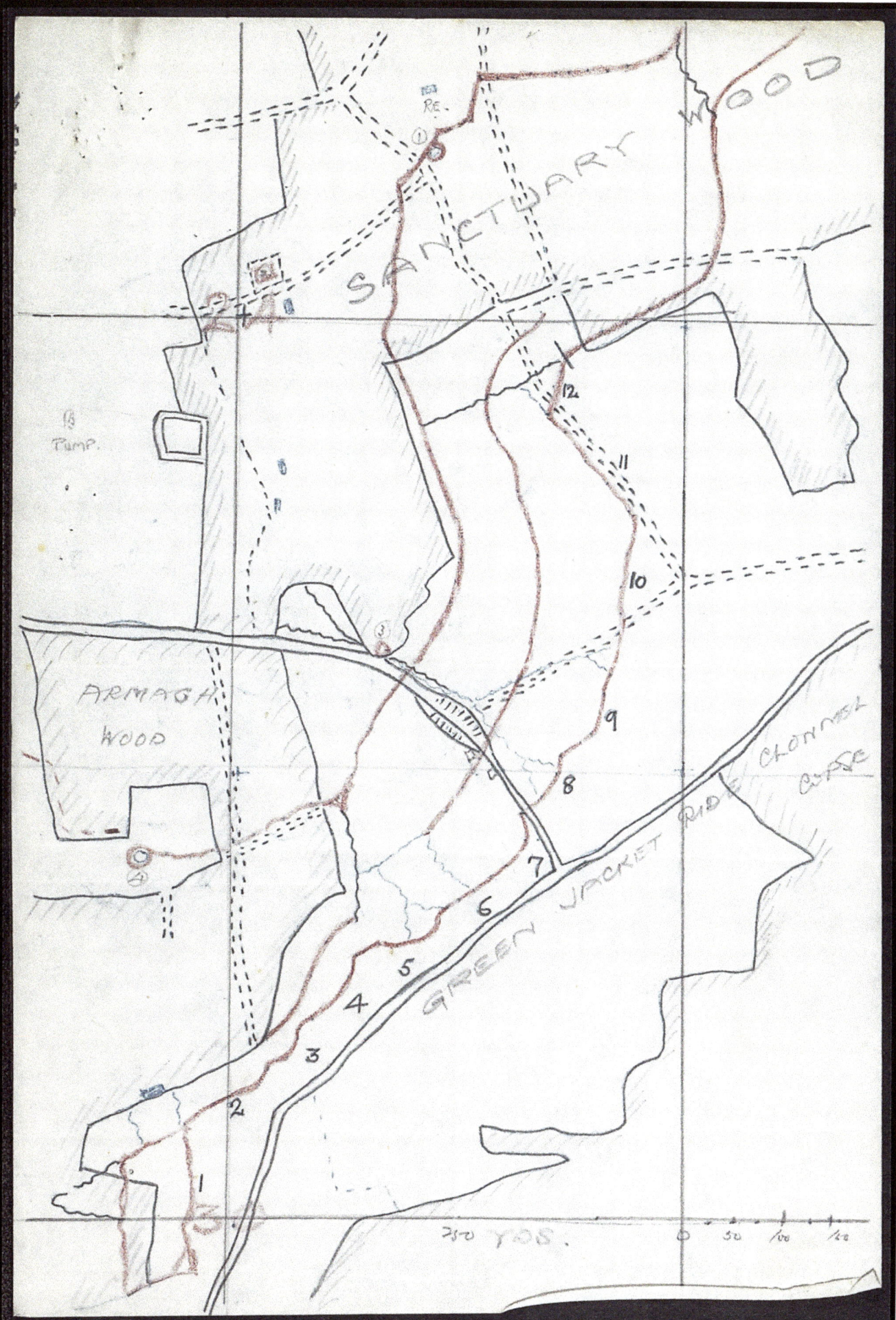

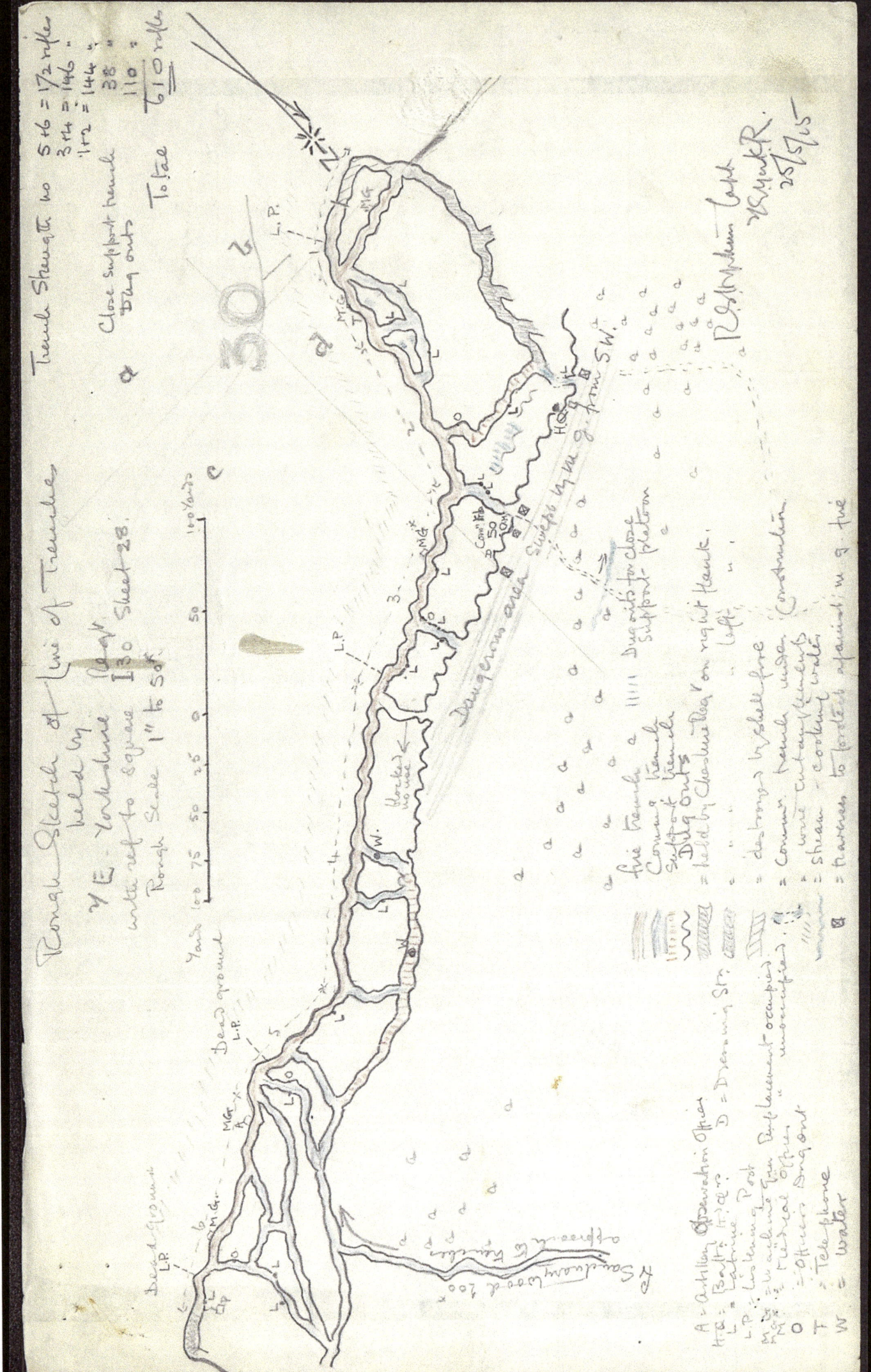

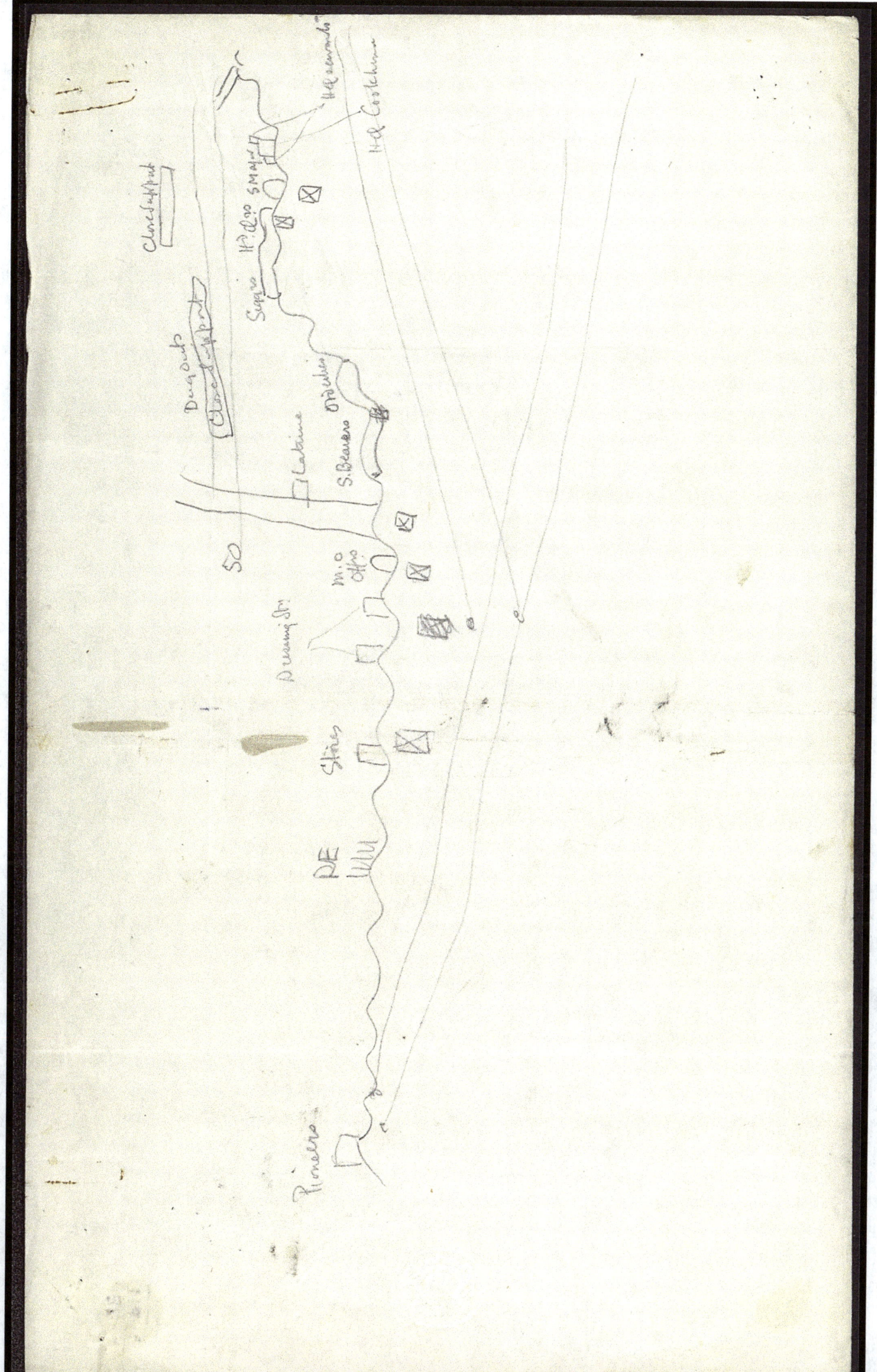

83rd Infantry Brigade.
28th Division.

WAR DIARY

2nd BATTN. EAST YORKSHIRE REGIMENT.

J U N E

1 9 1 5

On His Majesty's Service.

Army Form C. 2118

WAR DIARY
or
INTELLIGENCE SUMMARY
(Erase heading not required.)

Instructions regarding War Diaries and Intelligence Summaries are contained in F. S. Regs., Part II. and the Staff Manual respectively. Title Pages will be prepared in manuscript.

Place	Date	Hour	Summary of Events and Information	Remarks and references to Appendices
YPRES.	1.6.15		Quiet day. Officers Liverpool Scottish came to see trenches and two Officers of Indian Cavalry spent the night. Work going on well.	
—do—	2.6.15		A heavy bombardment by the Germans commenced at 2 p.m. Chiefly on the trenches held by the Cavalry on our Left ~~Right~~ which caught "A" & "C" Coys. Casualties however, slight. At night the Battalion was relieved by the Liverpool Scottish & marched by companies to "Hutments" S. of YLAMERTINGHE. Relief was accomplished just in time to get away under cover of darkness. The huts were reached at 4.45 a.m. 3.6.15. Casualties:- Killed 1. Wounded & Missing 1.	
VLAMERTINGHE	3.6.15	2 p.m.	Battalion marched at 2 p.m. via POPERINGHE and WATOU to WINNEZEELE, where it arrived at 7.45 p.m. A very trying march. Occupied same billetting area as on last occasion.	
WINNEZEELE	4.6.15		Cleaning up & resting. Draft of 49 arrived late at night.	

1875 Wt. W593/826 1,000,000 4/15 J.B.C. & A. A.D.S.S./Forms/C. 2118.

Army Form C. 2118

WAR DIARY
or
INTELLIGENCE SUMMARY

(Erase heading not required.)

Instructions regarding War Diaries and Intelligence Summaries are contained in F. S. Regs., Part II. and the Staff Manual respectively. Title Pages will be prepared in manuscript.

Place	Date	Hour	Summary of Events and Information	Remarks and references to Appendices
WINNEZEELE	5.6.15		BRIG. GEN. H.S.L. RAVENSHAW. C.M.G. inspected all drafts which had arrived during previous fortnight.	
—do—	6.6.15		Companies commenced programme of training. Following Officers joined :— MAJOR B.W. BOGLE. LIEUT. E.S. WILSON —"— W.E.C. WIEFALL.	
—do—	7.6.15		Training commenced. Weather very hot.	
—do—	8.6.15		Training.	
—do—	9.6.15		MAJOR B.W. BOGLE assumed command of the Battn. vice LIEUT. COL. W.H. YOUNG to England on leave. LIEUT. D.A. COX appointed Adjutant.	
—do—	10.6.15		Grenadier Platoons X and Y commenced training.	
—do—	11.6.15		Training	
—do—	12.6.15		—do—	

Army Form C. 2118

WAR DIARY
or
INTELLIGENCE SUMMARY
(Erase heading not required.)

Instructions regarding War Diaries and Intelligence Summaries are contained in F. S. Regs., Part II. and the Staff Manual respectively. Title Pages will be prepared in manuscript.

Place	Date	Hour	Summary of Events and Information	Remarks and references to Appendices
MINNEZEELE	13.6.15		Training	
—do—	14.6.15		Battalion left MINNEZEELE at 1 p.m. for Movement at LA CLYTTE.	
LA CLYTTE	15.6.15		Met KEMMEL arriving there at 7 p.m. Training	
—do—	16.6.15		—do—	
—do—	17.6.15		—do—	
—do—	18.6.15		—do—	
			No. 9303 Sergt. R. WHITE awarded the Distinguished Conduct Medal. The following is the action for which commended :— "On the forenoon of 8th May 1915, his Battn. advanced from the line to make an attack. On two occasions Sergt. WHITE took messages from the support trenches to the fire trenches under very heavy shell & rifle fire. On the second occasion he was wounded & although wounded volunteered to take a third message back for re-enforcements, again under fire. This message he successfully delivered. (63rd Bde. Order 38.5. of. 15.6.15)	

1875 Wt. W593/826 1,000,000 4/15 J.B.C. & A. A.D.S.S./Forms/C. 2118.

WAR DIARY
or
INTELLIGENCE SUMMARY

Army Form C. 2118

Place	Date	Hour	Summary of Events and Information	Remarks and references to Appendices
LA CLYTTE	18.6.15 (cont")		Lieut. J.L.I. HAWKESWORTH joined.	
KEMMEL	19.6.15		Brigade took over VIERSTRAAT - KEMMEL line of trenches. The Battn. relieved the 7th SHERWOOD FORESTERS. Relief completed by 12.45 a.m.	
- do -	20.6.15		Enemy's Trench Mortars caused several casualties in K.1. Trench (C. Coy.) Owing to defective telephone communication could not get supporting Batteries to take action till late in day. Casualties - Killed 4. Wounded 8. "A" Coy's reconnoitring patrol reported enemy's sap 70* from H.H. Trench. Our countermining from J. trenches still being carried on.	
- do -	21.7.15		At 9.15 p.m. a message came through from J.2. to say that H.H. had been mined and at 10 .30 relieved, occupied by the enemy. It was afterwards discovered that there was no cause for alarm as the mine had	

Army Form C. 2118

WAR DIARY
or
INTELLIGENCE SUMMARY
(Erase heading not required.)

Instructions regarding War Diaries and Intelligence Summaries are contained in F.S. Regs., Part II. and the Staff Manual respectively. Title Pages will be prepared in manuscript.

Place	Date	Hour	Summary of Events and Information	Remarks and references to Appendices
KEMMEL	22.6.15		Reported 50ˣ short of H.H. Battery 365 asked to open fire. 2 shells landed in enemy's trenches. Two of our patrols sent out in simultaneously to this effect and that the GERMANS were falling back into the PETIT BOIS WOOD. Companies opened rapid fire at time of guns opening fire, which it is hoped caused considerable loss to GERMANS. Casualties:- Killed 2. Wounded 4. Intermittent shelling. Patrols sent out as usual. Casualties:- Killed 3. Wounded 4. The undermentioned were mentioned in Despatches Gazette of 22.6.15.:- MAJOR. C.P. BERTHON. 2ⁿᵈ LIEUT. N.L.C. de RINZY. N° 6534 Sergt. H. PARKS. N° 6410 Coml Sergt. H. ROWLEY. N° 6439 Pte. N. OTTEWELL.	

Army Form C. 2118

WAR DIARY
or
INTELLIGENCE SUMMARY
(Erase heading not required.)

Instructions regarding War Diaries and Intelligence Summaries are contained in F.S. Regs., Part II. and the Staff Manual respectively. Title Pages will be prepared in manuscript.

Place	Date	Hour	Summary of Events and Information	Remarks and references to Appendices
KEMMEL	23.6.15		Salvo from heavy Battery NORTHUMBRIAN BDE on GERMAN working party in the PETIT BOIS WOOD by request of O.C. "A" Coy. Rendr Efford. B.W. casualties :- Wounded 2. 2nd LIEUT. N.L.C. de RINZY awarded the Military Cross of London Gazette 23.6.15.	
-do-	24.6.15		Handed over trenches to 1/K.O.Y.L.I. by 12.30. a.m. (25.6.15) and returned to Huttments at LA CLYTTE. Casualties :- Wounded 2.	
-do-	25.6.15		Huttments resting.	
-do-	26.6.15		-do- Casualties :- 1 man of working party wounded.	
-do-	27.6.15		-do- Casualties :- 1 man -do- -do-	
-do-	28.6.15		-do- -do- -do-	

Army Form C. 2118

WAR DIARY
or
INTELLIGENCE SUMMARY
(Erase heading not required.)

Instructions regarding War Diaries and Intelligence Summaries are contained in F. S. Regs., Part II. and the Staff Manual respectively. Title Pages will be prepared in manuscript.

Place	Date	Hour	Summary of Events and Information	Remarks and references to Appendices
KEMMEL	29.6.15		Relieved 1/ K.O.Y.L.I. in trenches by 11.45 p.m. "A" Coy. (Capt: FAWCETT), 5/ KING'S OWN, attached in H.1. & H.2. Casualties — Nil.	
-do-	30.6.15		Quiet day. "C" Coy. (Capt: EAVES), 5/ KING'S OWN, attached in H.5. Casualties during June 1915:— Officers Killed. Wounded. Missing Nil. Nil. Nil. Other ranks Killed Wounded Wounded & Missing 10 23 1 Casualties reported up to & for 30-6-15:— Officers Killed. Wounded. Missing 11 38 1 (6 since died) Other ranks Killed Wounded Missing 199 698 118.	

WAR DIARY
or
INTELLIGENCE SUMMARY
(Erase heading not required.)

Army Form C. 2118

Instructions regarding War Diaries and Intelligence Summaries are contained in F. S. Regs., Part II. and the Staff Manual respectively. Title Pages will be prepared in manuscript.

Place	Date	Hour	Summary of Events and Information	Remarks and references to Appendices
KEMMEL	30/6/15		Distribution of Battalion on 30-6-15.	

O.C.
Major B. W. Boyle.

2nd in Command.
Capt. R. S. Hopkins.

Adjutant   Lieut. D. A. Cox.
Qr. Mr.   Lieut. A. A. Henley.
Regt. Transport Officer   2nd Lieut. J. Webb.
Medical Officer Lieut. C. C. Hannson. R.A.M.C.

"A" Coy.
Lieut. T. R. Inglis (Leic. Reg.)

2/Lt. H. N. Williams (Yorkshire)
2/Lt. L. L. Banks (Yorkshire)
2/Lt. A. M. Merville (Yorkshire)
Other Ranks. 240

"B" Coy.
Lieut. V. Bristow (Leics.)
2/Lt. H.G. Sissons (3rd B.)
2/Lt. L.B. Frere (D.L.I.)
2/Lt. W.E.C. Wigfall (3rd Nor.)
2/Lt. F.A. Jenkins.
Other Ranks. 245

"C" Coy.
Lieut. E.S. Wilson
2/Lt. H.T. White
2/Lt. T.L. Barton (D.L.I.)
2/Lt. W.H. Greet (3rd Batt)
2/Lt. A. Crick (Leicester)
Other Ranks. 268

"D" Coy.
Lieut. J.L.I. Hartsworth
2/Lt. N.E. Trier
2/Lt. E.B. White
2/Lt. D.D. Anderson (3rd Battn.)
Other Ranks. 252.

Machine Gun Officer :- 2/Lieut. E.S. Reeves (3rd Batt.)

Army Form C. 2118

WAR DIARY
or
INTELLIGENCE SUMMARY
(Erase heading not required.)

Place	Date	Hour	Summary of Events and Information	Remarks and references to Appendices
			Total Strength :- Officers. W.O's. N.C.O's & Men = 1034. Grenadier Platoons :- Comdg. "X" Platoon. Comdg. "Y" Platoon. Lieut "H.A. Wilkinson. H. Lieut: C.E.H. Reckitt. Other ranks 50. (YORKSHIRE) Other ranks 50. Regtl. Sergt. Major. Regtl. Qr. Mr. Sergt. Orderly Room Sergt. Sgt. C. Williams G.W. Illing. P.W. Dominson. — do — Clerk. J.H. Potter. Coy. Sergt. Major. Coy. Qr. Mr. Sergt. A.E. Robinson. "C" G. Wottell. "D" E. Harborough. "A" J. Truepert. "C" C.M. Woodruffe. "B" R. Clifford. "A" B. Jeffcoat. "D" R. Petig. "B". (Acting) A.O.C attached Armr. St. Mr. Sgt. T. Lewis.	Signed [signature] Comm Major ...Rst 1/7/15

83rd Infantry Brigade.
28th Division.

WAR DIARY

2nd BATTN. EAST YORKSHIRE REGIMENT.

J U L Y

1 9 1 5

On His Majesty's Service.

WAR DIARY
or
INTELLIGENCE SUMMARY

(Erase heading not required.)

Army Form C. 2118

Place	Date	Hour	Summary of Events and Information	Remarks and references to Appendices
KEMMEL	1/7/15		Visited by the Divisional Commander, MAJ. GENERAL. E.S. BULFIN, C.V.O. Vigorous shelling in the afternoon and active artillery duel at	
		11 P.M.	night, commencing at 11 p.m. Wounded 8. (not including Lieut. C. Cornwallis.) Killed 1. HARRISON, R.A.M.C, Medical Officer to the Battalion, who was frozen on the cheek by a fragment of trench mortar.)	
-do-	3/7/15		Arrangements made for mutual co-operation with neighbouring units (Territorial Division on our right.) Company Officer reconnoitred from E. of Battn. Head Quarters. Battalion Staff Officer who sniped returning to Battalion Head Quarter & Lieut. C.E.H. RECKETTS was wounded in the face by a trench mortar.	

WAR DIARY
or
INTELLIGENCE SUMMARY

(Erase heading not required.)

Army Form C. 2118

Place	Date	Hour	Summary of Events and Information	Remarks and references to Appendices
KEMMEL	2/2/15 (cont?)		Special efforts called for from Division (by midnight note) to capture a German dead or alive. Patrols sent out could effect nothing to date. Casualties :- Wounded 1.	
- do -	3/2/15		Officers patrols sent out Commanded as follows :- K.1. Lieut: D.D. ANDERSON. D. Coy. (wounded) J.3. -do- H.G. DICKENS. B. -do- H.H. -do- H.R. WILKINSON. A. -do- Special patrols again sent out between 10 p.m. and 2 a.m. H.Y. 15. K.1. and J.3. Hundred attempts were but could effect nothing. Casualties :- Wounded 2.	

Army Form C. 2118

WAR DIARY
or
INTELLIGENCE SUMMARY
(Erase heading not required.)

Place	Date	Hour	Summary of Events and Information	Remarks and references to Appendices
KEMMEL	4/7/15		Patrol from H4 (Lieut: WILKINSON & 2 bombers) lay in ambush to catch a GERMAN listening patrol. Tired of waiting they found a GERMAN working party so threw a couple of bombs amongst them	
		2 A.M.	and returned at 2 a.m.	
			German patrol of 12 men seen by our listening patrol on night of 4/3. They opened fire and killed 1 German and the rest fled. Listening patrol consisted of :-	
			No. 18198 Pte. A. HARRISON. "B" Coy & No. 18189 Pte. J. WARD. "C" Coy	
			Casualties :- Wounded 4.	
-do-	5/7/15	11.00 a.m.	The following telegram was received from 83rd Brigade.	
			"B.M. 260 of 5/7/15. A G.O.C. 28th Division is very pleased with your success in getting the GERMAN last night and hopes the Brigade will get some more of them"	

Army Form C. 2118

WAR DIARY
or
INTELLIGENCE SUMMARY
(Erase heading not required.)

Place	Date	Hour	Summary of Events and Information	Remarks and references to Appendices
KEMMEL	5/7/15 (cont)	11.30 PM	Relieved by 11.30 p.m. by 1. K.O.Y.L.I. and proceeded to LA CLYTTE huts to rest. Casualties:- Wounded 2.	
LA CLYTTE	6/7/15		Battalion resting in huts at SCHERPENBERG	
-do-	7/7/15		—do—	
-do-	8/7/15		—do—	
-do-	9/7/15		—do—	
-do-	10/7/15		—do—	
KEMMEL	11/7/15		Relieved 1. K.O.Y.L.I. Quiet relief. "J" Trenches. Casualties:- Wounded 2.	
-do-	12/7/15		Re arrangement of trenches took place the YORK AND LANC. REG taking over "J" and the Battalion relieving the 5/LOYAL NORTH LANC. REG. in "G" trenches. Casualties:- Killed 1, Wounded 2.	

WAR DIARY
or
INTELLIGENCE SUMMARY
(Erase heading not required.)

Army Form C. 2118

Place	Date	Hour	Summary of Events and Information	Remarks and references to Appendices
KERNEL	13/7/15		Quiet day. Casualties: 2 Lieut. H.G. DICKENS & 5 men wounded.	
-do-	14/7/15		In evening sounds of enemy mining under C.1 heard. Expect	
		2.0 M	Sent for. At 8.10 p.m mine sent up. (3 distinct explosions). An orderly sent to YORK AND LANC. REG. Came back with negative information. Heavy rifle fire heard from trenches and Company in support ordered to "STAND TO".	
		9.15 PM	About 9.30 p.m. reported that a mine had been exploded in C.1. No enemy attack had apparently been made although some men said they saw GERMANS climbing over Allies' (enemy's) parapets.	
		9.30pm	At 9.30 p.m. 4 shrapnel dropped over SIEGE FARM and caught mining section as it was passing. Lieut. W.H.GREET and 12 men wounded.	

Army Form C. 2118

WAR DIARY
or
INTELLIGENCE SUMMARY
(Erase heading not required.)

Instructions regarding War Diaries and Intelligence Summaries are contained in F. S. Regs., Part II. and the Staff Manual respectively. Title Pages will be prepared in manuscript.

Place	Date	Hour	Summary of Events and Information	Remarks and references to Appendices
KEMMEL	14/15 (cont?)	9.40 p.m.	At 9.40 p.m. reported all quiet.	
		11 p.m.	At 11 p.m. the O.C. in Command (CAPT. R.S. HOPKINS) went up to G1 and inspected mine crater which was about 30' in diameter and 30' deep.	
			A. Coy. and 1 section of S.R.H at work, cutting trench through parapet which had been damaged by the explosion. Worked till dawn. Work half finished.	
			No interruption from enemy who were apparently repairing their Undetected by day owing to snipers and Machine Guns from SPANBROEK MOLEN.	
			Work continued next night by one platoon generation so as to hand over complete to relieving unit.	
			Casualties :- Killed (including those buried under debris) 13 Wounded 36.	

1875 Wt. W593/836 1,000,000 4/15 J.B.C. & A. A.D.S.S./Forms/C. 2118.

WAR DIARY
or
INTELLIGENCE SUMMARY

(Erase heading not required.)

Army Form C. 2118

Place	Date	Hour	Summary of Events and Information	Remarks and references to Appendices
KEMMEL	15/7/15		Took Officers of 6th LEICESTER REG. round our trenches and were relieved by that unit at night. Casualties :- Killed 1.	
LA CLYTTE	16/7/15	1.30 a.m.	Battalion all in at SCHERPENBERG huts by 1-30 a.m. Working party under LIEUT. L.B. FRERE (DURHAM L.I.) worked all night on destroyed parapet. Draft of 30 (Volunteers from Cavalry) joined. Ordered to be attached to 85 1/2 Brigade and took over billets from 5/ YORKSHIRE REG. AT LOCRE.	
LOCRE	17/7/15			
—do—	18/7/15	2.30 p.m.	At 2-30 p.m. the C.O., O.C Coys and Machine Gun Officer reconnoitred new line of trenches. "C", occupied by CANADIANS. Battalion moved out of LOCRE and occupied trenches at WULVERGHEM relieving 1st & 2nd Battn CANADIANS. A quiet night.	

Army Form C. 2118

WAR DIARY
or
INTELLIGENCE SUMMARY
(Erase heading not required.)

Place	Date	Hour	Summary of Events and Information	Remarks and references to Appendices
WOLVERGHEM	19/7/15		BRIG. GEN. C.E. PEREIRA (late COLDSTREAM GUARDS) Comdg. 85th Bde. taken round trenches by C.O. A quiet day except that 30 heavy shells fell in rear of "D" Coy. doing no damage. Patrols sent out at night found enemy working quietly. Sergeant BARNETT (No. Ex. 1819) was killed just as he was returning. He had done some excellent work and is a loss to the Battalion.	
		11.15 p.m.	At 11.15 p.m. a GERMAN working party was fired 5 rounds rapid by "A" Coy. Casualties – Killed 1. Wounded 2.	
do	20.7.15	12.5 a.m.	At 12.5 a.m. the GERMANS sent up a green star which was followed by a burst of fire from two fixed rifle batteries. Sniping becoming more vigorous. The 2nd in Command spent the night in the trenches. Patrols sent out from all Companies report enemy busy improving their own works.	

WAR DIARY
or
INTELLIGENCE SUMMARY

(Erase heading not required.)

Army Form C. 2118

Place	Date	Hour	Summary of Events and Information	Remarks and references to Appendices
WULVERGHEM	21/2/15		C.O. and 2nd in Command selected site for Hd.Qr. Battle Station. Very quiet day. Visited STRATHCONA'S HORSE on our right. Noted a long line of 1st line Transport drawn up in the open & large working parties. (see S.46)	
—do—	22/2/15		C.O. took G.O.C. 85th Brigade and Major BROWN, R.E. round trenches. Work being done approved, and decided to demolish ruins in front of "A" Coy. The A.D.M.S. (COLONEL N.C. FERGUSON, C.M.E.) and D.A.D.M.S. (LT. COL. H.S. ROCH) afterwards visited the trenches. The former said he was very pleased with all he saw and was impressed with the extraordinary cleanliness of the trenches. About a dozen big shells came over C.H. No damage done. Casualties:- Lieut. H.A. WILKINSON wounded & 1 killed & 1 wounded.	

Army Form C. 2118

WAR DIARY
or
INTELLIGENCE SUMMARY
(Erase heading not required.)

Instructions regarding War Diaries and Intelligence Summaries are contained in F. S. Regs., Part II. and the Staff Manual respectively. Title Pages will be prepared in manuscript.

Place	Date	Hour	Summary of Events and Information	Remarks and references to Appendices
WULVERGHEM	23/7/15	8 P.M.	A few shells came over from N.E. about 8 p.m.	
— do —	24/7/15		T.O. went round and selected a site for a rifle battery to fire on enemys dump 1300 x away.	
		2.30 P.M.	About 2.30 p.m. several shells came over C.1. (A Coy) and rifle grenades over C.4. (D.Coy). In the evening G.O.C. 28th Divn. visited Battn. Head Quarters. About 9.30 p.m. our guns sent over some three dozen shells. Enemy replied by shelling WULVERGHEM. Our 3rd 8″. took to their dugouts.	
— do —	25/7/15		Four enemy aeroplanes went over trenches. This was followed by rifle grenades in salvos of 3 and 5 over C.4 and C.5. No damage done. Night very quiet. Casualties :- Wounded 1.	

WAR DIARY
or
INTELLIGENCE SUMMARY
(Erase heading not required.)

Army Form C. 2118

Place	Date	Hour	Summary of Events and Information	Remarks and references to Appendices
WOLVERGHEM	26/5/		Enemy shelled the Head Quarters of the CANADIANS on our right in the morning & afternoon. Hot meals for the men sent up in Cookers as far as Battn. Hd. Qrs. as an experiment. Very satisfactory.	
- do -	27/5/		Officers of KING'S OWN taken round trenches. At 5 p.m. C.H. was shelled and our heavy artillery replied. Later enemy shelled C.3. Hot meals again sent up in Cookers. Casualties :- Killed 1. Wounded 1.	
- do -	28/5/	6.15 P.M.	About 8.15 p.m. enemy dropped 4 big shells within 100 x - 300 x of B² H² 8². No damage done. Hot meal again tonight. Casualties :- Wounded 1.	

Army Form C. 2118

WAR DIARY
or
INTELLIGENCE SUMMARY
(Erase heading not required.)

Place	Date	Hour	Summary of Events and Information	Remarks and references to Appendices
WULVERGHEM	29/7/15	9.45 P.M	Quiet morning. Canadian Head Qrs. (about 700x away) heavily shelled. Relief by 2/ KING'S OWN completed by 11.45 p.m. 2nd Battalion proceeded to LOCRE to billets.	
LOCRE	30/7/15		Resting in billets	

—do—	31/7/15		—do—
			2/Lts. T.N. BOWERBANK, E.G. WALLACE and A. WIGGINTON joined. Posted to "A", "B" and "C" Coys. respectively.
			Total sick wastage for July – 73 – 48 returned to duty – 14 evacuated to base.
			Casualties for month of July 1915:–
			    Officers
			  Killed Wounded Missing
			   Nil 3 Nil
			    Other ranks
			  Killed Wounded Missing
			   12 58 9.	

Army Form C. 2118

WAR DIARY
or
INTELLIGENCE SUMMARY
(Erase heading not required.)

Place	Date	Hour	Summary of Events and Information	Remarks and references to Appendices
			Casualties reported up to & for 31st July 1915:—	
			Officers	
			Killed Wounded Missing	
			1 4 & 3 1	
			(1 since died)	
			Other Ranks	
			Killed Wounded Missing	
			211 756 127.	
			[signature] Lieut Colonel,	
			17/8/15 Comm'g. 1/8 Mx Regt	

83rd Infantry Brigade.
28th Division.

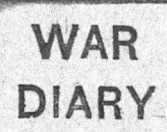

2nd BATTN. EAST YORKSHIRE REGIMENT.

A U G U S T

1 9 1 5

Sketch.

On His Majesty's Service.

Army Form C. 2118.

WAR DIARY
or
INTELLIGENCE SUMMARY.
(Erase heading not required.)

Instructions regarding War Diaries and Intelligence Summaries are contained in F.S. Regs., Part II. and the Staff Manual respectively. Title pages will be prepared in manuscript.

Hour, Date, Place	Summary of Events and Information	Remarks and references to Appendices
1/8/15 LOCRE	Resting in Billets	
	The following Officers having joined are posted to Cos. as stated:—	
	2/Lieut. T.N. BOWERBANK "A" Coy.	
	" G.E. WALLACE "B" Coy.	
	" A. WIGGINTON "C" Coy.	
2/8/15 —do—	Resting in Billets.	
3/8/15 —do—	Battalion moved into huts at SCHERPENBERG.	
4/8/15 SCHERPENBERG.	Battalion HEAD QUARTERS moved into farm E. of rnd. hereafter known as WHITE ROSE FARM.	
5/8/15 —do—	Battalion resting.	
	Draft of 40 joined.	
6/8/15 KEMMEL	Battalion relieved 1/ K.O.Y.L.I. in trenches "L" and "K" by 11.15 p.m. the 10th LANCASHIRE FUSILIERS	

WAR DIARY
or
INTELLIGENCE SUMMARY.

(Erase heading not required.)

Army Form C. 2118.

Hour, Date, Place	Summary of Events and Information	Remarks and references to Appendices
6/5/15 KEMMEL. (cont?)	(50th DIVN) being on our left. Battalion Head Qr. YORK HOUSE. Casualties :- Wounded 1. Quiet day. Enemy's snipers fairly active.	
7/5/15. KEMMEL.	The C.R.E. 38th Div. (MAJOR DOUGLAS) with CAPT. R.S. HOPKINS (SECOND IN COMMAND) selected sites for shell proof cover trenches and work started by all companies. Casualties :- Killed 1.	
2.40 a.m. 8/5/15 —do—	Our Artillery very active supporting an attack at HOOGE 3.40 a.m. Casualties :- Killed 1.	
7 a.m. 9/5/15 —do—	Quiet day. Casualties :- Wounded 1. Five Officers of LEICESTERSHIRE REG reported at B? Head Qrs at 9 a.m. and were then ordered to the trenches. In the evening the company to	

WAR DIARY
or
INTELLIGENCE SUMMARY.
(Erase heading not required.)

Army Form C. 2118.

Hour, Date, Place	Summary of Events and Information	Remarks and references to Appendices
9/5/15 KEMMEL (Cont.)	which they belonged was brought up and distributed among the trenches for instruction.	
10/5/15 KEMMEL	Quiet day. G.O.C. DIVN and BDE visited Battn. Hd Qrs. Enemy snipers active all night. New Company snipers selected 50 × in rear of "C" and "D" Coys to attack ration carriers supplies. Battle order for Battn Head Qrs selected. Casualties :- Killed 1. Wounded 1.	
11/5/15 —do—	Adjutant of LEIC. REG. thrown from his horse by G.O. In the running Coy of 6/ LEIC. REG. relieved by another Coy. Brigadier visited Battn Head Qrs at 5 p.m. Casualties :- Wounded 1.	

Army Form C. 2118.

WAR DIARY
or
INTELLIGENCE SUMMARY
(Erase heading not required.)

Instructions regarding War Diaries and Intelligence Summaries are contained in F. S. Regs., Part II. and the Staff Manual respectively. Title pages will be prepared in manuscript.

Hour, Date, Place	Summary of Events and Information	Remarks and references to Appendices
12/8/15. KEMMEL	Intermittent shelling by Enemy all day. Batt. relieved by 11. K.O.Y.L.I. and proceeded to SCHERPENBERG HUTS.	
13/8/15 SCHERPENBERG	Battalion resting	
14/8/15 — do —	— do —	
15/8/15 — do —	— do —	
16/8/15 — do —	— do —	
17/8/15 — do —	— do —	
10.25 p.m. 18/8/15 KEMMEL	Battalion relieved 11. K.O.Y.L.I. Relief completed by 10.25 p.m. the quickest relief to date.	
19/8/15 — do —	Quiet day and night. "A", "B", & "C" Coys. in trenches. Brigadier and Brig. General W.T. FURSE, C.B., D.S.O. O. Spent night in trenches. Visited by Brigadier.	
20/8/15 — do —	Quiet day & night. 2/Lieut: R.J.H. GATRELL joined and attached to GRENADIER PLATOON. Casualties:- Wounded 3.	

WAR DIARY
or
INTELLIGENCE SUMMARY.
(Erase heading not required.)

Army Form C. 2118.

Instructions regarding War Diaries and Intelligence Summaries are contained in F.S. Regs., Part II and the Staff Manual respectively. Title pages will be prepared in manuscript.

Hour, Date, Place	Summary of Events and Information	Remarks and references to Appendices
21/8/15 KEMMEL	Very wet morning. Brigadier went all round trenches 6 - 10.30 p.m. Started hot mid-day meal to trenches - worked very well and much appreciated. 2/Lieut. G.H.B. BOLTON joined and posted to "A" Coy.	
22/8/15 —do—	Quiet day. Usual intermittent shelling. Casualties :- Killed 1.	
23/8/15 —do—	G.O.C. visited Batt: Head Qrs in the evening. Our Howitzer Battery bombarded trenches in front of the "M²"	
10.10 p.m 24/8/15 —do—	Heavy shelling now of the afternoon & evening. Relieved by 1/. K.O.Y.L.I. 10-10 p.m. & proceeded to SCHERPENBERG HUTS.	
25/8/15 SCHERPENBERG	Resting in huts.	

Army Form C. 2118.

WAR DIARY
or
INTELLIGENCE SUMMARY

(Erase heading not required.)

Instructions regarding War Diaries and Intelligence Summaries are contained in F. S. Regs., Part II. and the Staff Manual respectively. Title pages will be prepared in manuscript.

Hour, Date, Place	Summary of Events and Information	Remarks and references to Appendices
26/8/15. SCHERPENBERG	Resting in huts.	
27/8/15 — do —	— do —	
28/8/15 — do —	Whole Battⁿ employed on Subsidiary Line.	
29/8/15. — do —	Resting in huts. Casualties :- Wounded 1.	
8 p.m. 30/8/15. — do —	G.O.C. 2nd Army (LIEUT. GENERAL SIR H.C.O. PLUMER, K.C.B.) inspected the Battalion at 3 p.m. He expressed himself pleased with everything he saw. He was accompanied by Major General E.S. BULFIN, C.V.O, C.B. Comdg. 28th Divⁿ. Battalion occupied the same trenches in the evening. Casualties :- Wounded 1.	
31/8/15. KEMMEL	Quiet day. Casualties :- Wounded 1.	

Army Form C. 2118.

WAR DIARY
or
INTELLIGENCE SUMMARY

(Erase heading not required.)

Instructions regarding War Diaries and Intelligence Summaries are contained in F. S. Regs., Part II. and the Staff Manual respectively. Title pages will be prepared in manuscript.

Hour, Date, Place	Summary of Events and Information	Remarks and references to Appendices

Casualties for August 1915.

Officers — Other Ranks

Killed. Wounded. Missing. Killed. Wounded. Missing.
Nil   Nil   Nil   3   11   Nil

Casualties Reported to 31st August 1915.

Officers

Killed Wounded Missing
  11   43   1
       (1 since died)

Other Ranks

Killed Wounded Missing
 314   767   137.

Major ? R?
? ?
Comdg ?

Secret: "C" Trenches.

Trench.	Garrisons.	Found By.
C.1.*	2½ Platoons.	A Coy.
C.2.	1 "	½ in Support Five Trenches
C.1.S.	½ "	
R.2.*	1 Coy.	B. Coy.
L.2.*	3 Platoons	
C.3.*	1 "	C. Coy.
C.3.S.	2 "	
C.4.*	1 "	D Coy.
C.4.S.	½ "	
S.P.4	1 "	
Souvenir F^m	1 "	Grenadiers.
— do —	1 "	— do —
— do —	½ "	

Scale 5000
200 100 50 0 200 400 yards

The Officer Commanding
   the Depôt
East Yorkshire Regiment.

83rd Infantry Brigade.
28th Division.

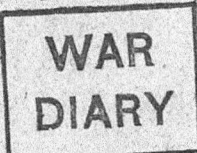

2nd BATTN. EAST YORKSHIRE REGIMENT.

S E P T E M B E R

1 9 1 5

Appendices.

On His Majesty's Service.

WAR DIARY
or
INTELLIGENCE SUMMARY

(Erase heading not required.)

Army Form C. 2118

CONFIDENTIAL

War Diary
of
2/ East Yorkshire Regt.

From 1st Sept. 1915 to 30th Sept. 1915

CONFIDENTIAL

2/EAST YORKSHIRE REGT.

WAR DIARY or **INTELLIGENCE SUMMARY**

(Erase heading not required.)

Army Form C. 2118

Page 1

Instructions regarding War Diaries and Intelligence Summaries are contained in F.S. Regs., Part II. and the Staff Manual respectively. Title Pages will be prepared in manuscript.

Place	Date	Hour	Summary of Events and Information	Remarks and references to Appendices
K' east L trenches	Sept 1st		Trenches - nothing to report	
"	2nd		" " "	
"	3		" " "	
"	4th		" " " Casualties during tour 1 killed 3 wounded	
SCHERPENBERG	5th		Relieved by 1st K.O.Y.L.I. and proceeded to WHITE ROSE FARM, SCHERPENBERG.	
"	6th		Enemy dropped 15. 5.9 percussion Shrapnel on SCHERPENBERG - one only landed near the Windmill and one through G.O.C.'s hut dug out. Lt. Col. W. A. BLAKE D.S.O. 1st Wilts Regt. arrived and took over command of the Battalion.	
"	7th			
"	8th		Resting - nothing to report	
"	9th		" " "	
"	10th		" " "	
K & L trenches	11th		Relieved 1st K.O.Y.L.I. in the trenches (K & L trenches) distribution as follows K1 new, K1 E, K2, K2a } B Coy K2 E, L1 new, L6, L2 } A Coy L3, L4, L5, L7 E } D Coy K3, L7 r, L1 } grenadiers - C Coy in reserve no casualties	

Army Form C. 2118
Page 2

WAR DIARY
or
INTELLIGENCE SUMMARY
(Erase heading not required.)

Place	Date	Hour	Summary of Events and Information	Remarks and references to Appendices
K 4 L trenches	Sept 12th		Quiet day. Weather fine. Wind N.E. Started building cooking places with a view to using camp kettles. First FRERIE beyond from enemy of distinction in bombing near CASSELS in casualties.	
"	13th		Hot Sun. Wind varying from N.E. to West. Quiet day. No casualties. Visited by Major NEEDHAM G.S.O. 28th Div. in afternoon and by Br. Gen. RAVENSHAW.	
"	14th		Hot day - Wind S.W. Quiet day. No casualties. Arranges for new rifle batteries near WATLING STREET and the FOSSE.	
"	15th		Dull & warm - Wind S.W. Quiet day - one man killed. Showery in the evening.	
"	16th		Dull & warm - Wind S.W. Quiet day - Enemy observed building a redoubt E of PETIT BOIS - one man wounded. (Slight)	
"	17th		Dull & warm - Wind S.W. Veering to N.W. Relieved by 1st K.O.Y.L.I. Relief completed 9.45 p.m.	

Army Form C. 2118

WAR DIARY
or
INTELLIGENCE SUMMARY
(Erase heading not required.)

Page 3

Place	Date	Hour	Summary of Events and Information	Remarks and references to Appendices
SCHERPENBERG	Sept 18		Resting. Hot wind. N.	
"	19	10 a.m.	Church parade. Major BOGLE returned off leave	
"	20		Fine & hot. Usual parades	
"	21		" " "	
"	22		" " "	
OUTERSTEENE	23		Marched to OUTERSTEENE where Battalion was billeted. In BAILLEUL Battalion marched past the Corps Commander Sir CHARLES FERGUSSON. Started 9.20 a.m. and reached billets 12 noon. Hot & tiring march. Lieut. W. BUXTON returned from Mt NOIR.	
"	24		Hot & stuffy. Wind S. Route march and physical exercises. 2nd Lieut. BARKAS returned off leave	

WAR DIARY
or
INTELLIGENCE SUMMARY
(Erase heading not required.)

Army Form C. 2118

Page 4

Place	Date	Hour	Summary of Events and Information	Remarks and references to Appendices
ROBECQ	Sept 26th		Marched from OUTERSTEENE to ROBECQ. Started at 5 a.m - reached ROBECQ at 12.30 p.m. - halted there 1½ hours and marched at 2 p.m. in direction of M¹ BERNENCHUN. Battalion was halted here and marched back again to Billets at ROBECQ. The day was fine and hot.	
NOYELLES	27th		Entrained at 12.30 p.m. and moved through BETHUNE to NOYELLES Battalion bivouaced in a field close to NOYELLES H.Q. It rained hard during the afternoon.	
	28th		At 3 a.m. Battalion moved to VERMELLES and came under orders of 22nd Brigade. From VERMELLES a staff officer led the Battalion into reserve trenches near 22nd Brigade Hdqrs. Then the Battalion spent the day from 5 a.m to 6 p.m. shelling in three trenches was fairly frequent throughout the day resulting in 5 casualties Lieut V. BUXTON was wounded with shrapnel. In the evening B & C Coys moved into trenches W of QUARRY and took over trenches from R. SCOTS & MIDDLESEX Relief completed 2 a.m	

WAR DIARY
or
INTELLIGENCE SUMMARY
(Erase heading not required.)

Army Form C. 2118.

Page 3"

Place	Date	Hour	Summary of Events and Information	Remarks and references to Appendices
	Sept 29th		About 7 a.m. Enemy started a bombing attack along St ELIE trench. Lieu Squadt Grenadiers under Lieut FREKE were despatched to reinforce S. Staffords. They did good work and succeeded in beating off the attack. At 9 a.m. Enemy broke through the Buffs on Battlewiliff and commenced a strong bombing attack which affected our left Company (C.Co.) Lieut FREKE with his bombers succeeded in beating off this attack and occupied trenches left vacant by the Buffs. During the attack Capt. E.S. WILSON and Lieut. L.B. FRERE were killed & Lieut J.A. JENKINS wounded. About 90 men of 'C' Company became casualties. In the afternoon Germans again attacked heavily with bombers and bombed the Middlesex out of their trenches on the left of our line in BIG WILLIE. Lieut R.J.H. GATRELL counterattacked with two squads of bombers and retook the whole of the line taken by the Germans which the Middlesex reoccupied. In the evening D Coy. relieved C on the left of the line and 'A' Coy and the remains of C took over a new piece of line from the S.Staffords Queens and Warwicks. The day was a bad one.	

Army Form C. 2118

WAR DIARY
or
INTELLIGENCE SUMMARY
(Erase heading not required.)

Page 6

Place	Date	Hour	Summary of Events and Information	Remarks and references to Appendices

	Sept 30th		Fine day. Bombing Germans started on our left. This attack made no progress as all the Communication trenches had been thoroughly blocked by being filled in.
			 2/Lieut R.J.H. GATRELL was wounded in the morning.
			
			 Casualties for September 1915
			   Killed Officers wounded missing
			   2 3 NIL
			   Killed Other ranks wounded missing
			   24 90 6
			
			 Casualties reported 1 to 30th September 1915
			   Killed Officers wounded missing
			   13 46 1
			     (7 since died)
			   Killed Other ranks wounded missing
			   238 857 133
			
			 10.10.15
			
			 A. Beaver, Lt Col
			 Cmdg 2/East Yorkshire Regt.	

APPENDICES.

"A" Form. Army Form C. 2121.
MESSAGES AND SIGNALS.   No. of Message

Prefix	Code	m.	Words	Charge	This message is on a/c of:	Recd. at	m.
Office of Origin and Service Instructions.			80			Date	
	2 V		Sent At m. To By	Coby Service. (Signature of "Franking Officer.")	From By	

TO | Second East Yorks | Urgent |

| Sender's Number. | Day of Month | In reply to Number | |
| * BM 939 | 28 | | A A A |

Your	Battalion	will	be	required
to	take	over	the German	trenches
this	evening	from	the	13th
Middlesex	and	9th	S.R Scots	from
G 5 C	10.4 to	A 5 A	6.0	A A A
Garrison	two	Companies	A.A.A	Time
of	relief	notified	later	but
not	before	6 pm	A A A	Officers
to be	sent	forthwith	to	see
trenches	A A A	If	these	Officers will
call	at	Bde H.Q	on	their
way	down	They	will	be
directed	as	to	routes	

From 22 Inf Bde
Place
Time 3.20 PM (Sd) F A H Thorboro Major
The above may be forwarded as now corrected. (Z) B.M.
Censor. Signature of Addressor or person authorised to telegraph in his name.
* This line should be erased if not required.

"A" Form. Army Form C. 212.
MESSAGES AND SIGNALS. No. of Message

Prefix	Code	m.	Words	Charge	This message is on a/c of:	Recd. at	m.
Office of Origin and Service Instructions.			Sent			Date	
			At		Service.	From	
			To		(Signature of "Franking Officer.")	By	
			By				

TO 27ᵗʰ Bd.

Sender's Number.	Day of Month	In reply to Number		A A A
EY 354	28			

The Germans are now shelling
our bombing counterattack with heavy
howitzer shells. A.A.A. Suggest German
observation posts be shelled

From O.C. E York
Place
Time
*The above may be forwarded as now corrected.   (Z)   (sd) W.B
Censor.   Signature of Addressor or person authorised to telegraph in his name.
*This line should be erased if not required.

"A" Form.   Army Form C. 2121.
MESSAGES AND SIGNALS.   No. of Message

TO   22nd Bde

Sender's Number | Day of Month | In reply to Number | | AAA
* BY 353 | 29 | | |

Germans appear to be congregating
N of FOSSE No 8
and houses in vicinity AAA
from these points they have
made several attacks AAA I
have broken up these with
M G but think some shrapnel
there would be valuable AAA
Situation on left of my
line is still a bit
Confused.

From O.C 2 E YORKs
Place
Time

"A" Form.
MESSAGES AND SIGNALS.   Army Form C. 2121.
                                          No. of Message_____

Prefix____ Code____ m. Words | Charge   This message is on a/c of: Recd. at_____ m.
Office of Origin and Service Instructions.   Date_____
_____   Sent   _____Service.   From_____
                        At____ 6.0 __ m. 19
                        To____   By_____
                        By____   (Signature of "Franking Officer.")

TO | 22nd Bde | | | |

Sender's Number.	Day of Month	In reply to Number	AAA
FY 355	29		
Situation	here	is	much	more
favourable	Enemy	have	been	driven
back	up	SLAG	ALLEY	and
this	trench	is	being	blocked
AAA	We	are	still	being
rather	heavily	shelled	about	point
59	59	5 D	by	heavy
German	howitzers	AAA	My	bombing
officer	has	been	wounded	and
many	of	the	regtl	Bombers

From O C 2E YORKS
Place
Time   The above may be forwarded as now corrected.   (Z) (sd) H.B.
                                    Censor.   Signature of Addressor or person authorised to telegraph in his name.
       * This line should be erased if not required.

"A" Form. Army Form C. 2121.
MESSAGES AND SIGNALS.

Prefix	Code	m.	Words	Charge	This message is on a/c of:	Recd. at _____ m.
Office of Origin and Service Instructions.			Sent			Date
			At _____ m.		Copy _____ Service.	From
			To			
			By		(Signature of "Franking Officer.")	By

TO	22nd I.B.			

Sender's Number.	Day of Month	In reply to Number		AAA
* EY 351	29			
Situation	here	appears	confused	AAA
Germans	made	a	heavy	bombing
attack	down	ST	ELIE	but
were	driven	back	300	yards
AAA	On	left	a	heavy
bombing	attack	is	proceeding	I
have	just	met	parties	of
BUFFS	who	said	that	they
had	received	orders	from	an
officer	to	retire	AAA	the
YORK	and	LANCS	are	trying
to	relieve	BUFFS	but	trench
is	very	congested	AAA	I
have	sent	a	strong	bombing
party	to	assist	BUFFS	bombers
who	I	understand	are	there
AAA	My	own	line	is

From
Place
Time

The above may be forwarded as now corrected. (Z)

Censor. Signature of Addressor or person authorised to telegraph in his name.

* This line should be erased if not required.

"A" Form.   Army Form C. 2121.

MESSAGES AND SIGNALS.

			AAA
ntact	AAA	all bombs	here
are	exhausted	and we	are
at	present	using German	ones
AAA	I	think a	supply
of	500	bombs are	necessary
at	once	and this	amount
should	be	supplied daily	both
for	SLAG	ALLEY and	ST
ELIE			

From: O C E YORKS

"A" Form.
Army Form C. 2121.

MESSAGES AND SIGNALS.

Prefix	Code	m.	Words	Charge	This message is on a/c of:	Recd. at	m.
Office of Origin and Service Instructions.							
			Sent		Copy Service.	Date	
			At	m.		From	
			To				
			By		(Signature of "Franking Officer.")	By	

| TO | CAPT HEAPS | | |
| | | MIDDLESEX | |

| Sender's Number. | Day of Month | In reply to Number | | AAA |
| EY 2 | 29 | | | |

Can	you	hold	junction	of
Reach 6	at	point	35	Sq
G	5	a	and	erect
30	to	40	yards	barricade
beyond	junction	to	prevent	enemy
bombing	up	AAA	If	enemy
in	possession	of	S	FACE
from	point	35	to	point
60	Sq	G	4	b
AAA	Information	urgently	required	AAA
If	unoccupied	please	state	AAA
sandbags	are	being	sent	up

From	O.C. E YORKS		
Place			
Time			

The above may be forwarded as now corrected. **(Z)**

Censor. Signature of Addressor or person authorised to telegraph in his name.

* This line should be erased if not required.

(C32) —McC. & Co. Ltd., London.— W 11400-2045. 100,000 2/15. Forms C 2121/10.

"A" Form.
Army Form C. 2121.
MESSAGES AND SIGNALS.
No. of Message

TO: O.C. EAST YORKS

I	cannot	hold	junction	of
trench	at	point	95	is
South	FACE	junction	of	trench
at	point	95	X	about
250ˣ	of	this	trench	are
occupied	by	Germans		
			I am	building
a	barricade	but	it	is
a	slow	job	Thanks	for
Sandbags				

(Sd) E A Heaps Capt
O.C. Middl Regt

"A" Form.
Army Form C. 2121.
MESSAGES AND SIGNALS.

Prefix	Code	m.	Words	Charge		This message is on a/c of:		Recd. at	m.
Office of Origin and Service Instructions.			Sent			Copy	Service.	Date	
			At	m.				From	
			To			(Signature of "Franking Officer.")		By	
			By						

TO | 83 Inf Bde | | |

Sender's Number.	Day of Month	In reply to Number		AAA
* EY 366	30			

I	have	just	returned	from
a	lengthy	tour	of	trenches
from	ST	ELIE	AVENUE	to
point	35	at	junction	of
S	FACE	and	main	line
German	trenches	AAA	There	is
still	a	medley	of	units
in	our	line	they	run
as	follows	from	Right	to
Left	KINGS	OWN	E YORKS	2
platoons	YORK	and	LANCS	50
men	MIDDLESEX	three	platoons	KOYLI
B	Coy	YORK	and	LANCS
D	Coy	YORK	and	LANCS
then	KOYLI	AAA	As	far
as	I	can	make	out
we	hold	to	beyond	point

From
Place
Time

The above may be forwarded as now corrected. (Z)
Censor. Signature of Addressor or person authorised to telegraph in his name.
* This line should be erased if not required.

"A" Form.
MESSAGES AND SIGNALS.
Army Form C. 2121.

35	and	SOUTH	FACE	but
the	Officers	Commanding	Coys	their
were	quite	uncertain	what	they
were	holding	~~...~~	~~...~~	~~...~~
~~...~~	~~...~~	~~...~~	~~...~~	~~...~~
~~...~~	~~...~~	~~...~~	~~...~~	~~...~~
~~...~~	~~...~~	~~...~~	~~...~~	~~...~~
~~...~~	~~...~~	AAA	Situation	here
is	quiet	and	there	is
a	plentiful	supply	of	bombs
AAA	The	Germans	are	busy
digging	a	redoubt	to	N
of	SLAG	ALLEY	point	G5a
8.4	close	to	our	line
I	think	an	Artillery	observing

"A" Form.
MESSAGES AND SIGNALS.

Army Form C. 2121.

officer	should	be	sent	up
and	some	heavy	howitzer	shells
dropped	on	it	before	it
is	too	late	AAA	I
will	send	you	a	rough
sketch	of	positions	during	the
day	AAA	the	"Stoll"	require
much	more	stokes	boards	pickets
corrugated	iron	sandbags	to	make
the	trenches	properly	tenable	AAA
Our	front	trench	is	still
very	shallow	and	men	get
badly	sniped	from	the	SLAG
HEAP	AAA	I	should	like
some	D5	cable	in	addition
to	other	requirements		

From: O C E YORKS
Place:
Time: 10.15 AM

"A" Form.
MESSAGES AND SIGNALS.
Army Form C. 2121.

Prefix	Code	m.	Words	Charge	This message is on a/c of:	Recd. at	m.
Office of Origin and Service Instructions.		Sent		Service.	Date	
		At	m.	Copy	From	
		To		(Signature of "Franking Officer.")	By	
		By				

TO: 2/E YORKS

| Sender's Number. | Day of Month | In reply to Number | | |
| BM 957 | 29 | | | A A A |

Orders received from 28TH DIV
that the Coy of MIDDLESEX
must be put back in
its original position AAA If
unable to do this by
itself it must be assisted
by EAST YORKS REGT AAA
addressed 3RD MIDDLESEX REGT 2/EAST
YORKS AAA acknowledge

From: 22 INF BDE
Place:
Time: 6.15 PM

"A" Form.
MESSAGES AND SIGNALS.
Army Form C. 2121.

TO: 2 East Yorkshire Regt

Sender's Number	Day of Month	In reply to Number	
*BM 618	15	5	AAA

Instruct Northumberland Fusiliers advancing your left who are not off from their own battalion as follows AAA A small attack is being launched against LITTLE WILLIE at 5 PM RWL Commander wishes Northumberland Fusiliers to hold on and clear all Germans out of BM WILLIE before dawn AAA They should take every advantage of confusion caused by above attack AAA Addressed 2/E. Yorks Regt repeated 84th Bde

From: 83 Brigade
Place:
Time: 6.54 PM

(Z)

83rd Infantry Brigade.
28th Division.

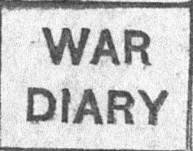

2nd BATTN. EAST YORKSHIRE REGIMENT.

OCTOBER

1915

Appendices:

O.O. 22 &
B.M. 644.

On His Majesty's Service.

Volume No. 1.

9.F.
In sheets

121.
Med 1
619

MEDITERRANEAN EXPEDITIONARY FORCE.

28th Div France

WAR DIARY.

Unit 2nd Bn. East Yorks Regt

From 1st October 1915 To 31st Octr 1915.

2/ E Yorks left France
for East Mediterranean.
Joined 28th Div on 27/10/15

abortive attempt to attack
Hohenzollern Redoubt on 4/10/15
which failed (see Reports)

Army Form C. 2118

WAR DIARY
or
INTELLIGENCE SUMMARY
(Erase heading not required.)

Instructions regarding War Diaries and Intelligence Summaries are contained in F. S. Regs., Part II. and the Staff Manual respectively. Title Pages will be prepared in manuscript.

CONFIDENTIAL

WAR DIARY
of
2ND EAST YORKSHIRE REGT.

From 1st October 1915 to 31st October 1915

Place	Date	Hour	Summary of Events and Information	Remarks and references to Appendices

WAR DIARY
or
INTELLIGENCE SUMMARY

Army Form C. 2118

Place	Date	Hour	Summary of Events and Information	Remarks and references to Appendices
nr HULLUCH	October 1st		Fine and warm. In the trenches. Relieved by 8th Kings Liverpool Regt in the evening. Relief complete by 5 am 2nd. Returned to ANNEQUIN.	
ANNEQUIN	2nd		Spent the day and night in billets at ANNEQUIN	
nr HULLUCH	3rd		Moved off from ANNEQUIN at 11am to relieve 2nd Cheshire Regt and Suffolks in the trenches. Relief complete 7pm. The trenches were immediately South of HOHENZOLLERN redoubt.	
	4th	At 8pm	A having evening received orders that a combined attack of 2 E. York. R. and 11 KOYLI was to be made on HOHENZOLLERN.	B.M. 644 v. Operation Orders for y Bde w/ & German attacks
		4.15am	Bombardment was to start at 4.15am lasting until 4.45am when the attack was to be launched. At 4.20am 'B' Company were to	
		4.20am	Captain W.H. WILSON moved out as ordered and took up a position about 50 yards in front of our trenches preparatory to moving forward after the bombardment. Heavy rifle and M.G. fire was opened by the enemy and the Company was unable to advance. Given at that [idirect?] direction.	
		4.45am	At 4.45am 'B' Company rose and charged forward but were immediately mown down by an intense rifle and M.G. fire. 'D' Company who were 91. kgs. followed 'B' were unable to more owing to the congestion in the trenches consequent on 'B' Company being unable to make ground.	

WAR DIARY
or
INTELLIGENCE SUMMARY

Army Form C. 2118

Place	Date	Hour	Summary of Events and Information	Remarks and references to Appendices
HULLUCH	October 4		(continued) K.O.Y.L.I. on our left suffered severely in a similar manner & attribute failure of the attack to following causes:- (1) the artillery bombardment. (2) Complete lack of element of surprise. The Germans were well prepared and had not been in the slightest shaken by the Artillery shelling that had taken place throughout the day. (3) The Germans had been digging themselves in during the day previous and had thoroughly improved their trenches. (4) The relief the day before did not finish until 7 p.m. Company officers had only a very indistinct idea of the trenches they were occupying and none at all of the position they were to attack. Two thirds of the leading Company became Casualties, including Captain W. H. WILSON (Yorkshire Regt) Killed. See Lieut N. E. TRIER and Lieut A. WIGGINGTON wounded. See Lieut N. E. TRIER died of wounds on 6th October. During the evening wiring in front of the trenches of the K.O.Y.L.I. was continued. As the enemy's rifle fire was fairly continuous a few Casualties occurred.	wiped out [?] enemy
"		3-4	Desultory shelling by Germans throughout the day. Chiefly Field Guns. Relieved by Irish and Scots Guards in evening. Relief completed 5 a.m. following morning.	

WAR DIARY
or
INTELLIGENCE SUMMARY

(Erase heading not required.)

Army Form C. 2118

Instructions regarding War Diaries and Intelligence Summaries are contained in F.S. Regs., Part II. and the Staff Manual respectively. Title Pages will be prepared in manuscript.

Place	Date	Hour	Summary of Events and Information	Remarks and references to Appendices
ANNEQUIN	October 6th	5 a.m.	Marched to ANNEQUIN. Halted from 5 a.m. to 1 p.m. Then marched to LES HARISOIRS where the Battalion went into rest billets. Fine but dull.	
#LES HARISOIRS	7th		Rest day. Battalion spent day cleaning up, and counting deficiencies in kit &c. Draft of nine Officers and sixty six arrived. Fine but dull.	
	8th		Commenced detailed programme of work. Rents hay from particular billets in was paid to reorganising Battalion. 9 a.m. to 11 a.m. Major B.W. BOGLE 5th Batt. Northumberland Fusiliers (late Adjutant) (84th Brigade) Command of Battalion. Programme of work continued.	
	9th		2 p.m. G.O.C. 28th Division visited the Battalion.	
	10th		Fine. Church parades. Other parades as usual.	
	11th		Usual parades.	
	12th		"	
	13th		Brigade parades for new Divisional Commander Maj. Gen. BRIGGS. Usual parades.	
	14th			
ESSARS	15th		Moved to ESSARS and took over billets from Yorkshire Regt.	
	16th		Fine. day spent in cleaning of billets.	
PREOL	17th		Fine. Moved to PREOL. Day spent in cleaning of billets.	

WAR DIARY
or
INTELLIGENCE SUMMARY
(Erase heading not required.)

Summary of Events and Information

Casualties for October 1915

Officers			Other ranks		
killed	wounded	missing	killed	wounded	missing
1	4*	0	29	101	4

*1 since died of wounds

Casualties reported to 31st October 1915

Officers			Other ranks		
killed	wounded	missing	killed	wounded	missing
14	50✱	1	267	958	137

✱ 8 since died of wounds

CheSeates
Lt. Col.
Comdg 2/East Yorkshire Regt.

Army Form C. 2118

WAR DIARY
or
INTELLIGENCE SUMMARY
(Erase heading not required.)

Instructions regarding War Diaries and Intelligence Summaries are contained in F. S. Regs., Part II. and the Staff Manual respectively. Title Pages will be prepared in manuscript.

Place	Date	Hour	Summary of Events and Information	Remarks and references to Appendices
PREOL	October 18th		Fine. Usual parades.	
"	19th		"	
"	20th		"	
LENGLET	21st		Fine. Moved to LENGLET. About 9 miles march.	
"	22nd		Left LENGLET on night of 22nd. Marched to FOUQUEREUIL Railway Station.	
L.U. train	23rd		Entrained at 1.30 a.m.	
"	24th		On train	
MARSEILLES	25th		Reaches MARSEILLES at 7am and obtains there. Marches to quay 4½ miles reaching ship at 12.30 p.m. Troops embarked on S/S. MALDA (Batt'n H.Qrs. and 2 Companies) and on S/S ALNWICK CASTLE. Remained in MARSEILLES. For the night. Regimental Transport left in camp in MARSEILLES.	
"	26th		Rain throughout the day. Day spent on the ships in MARSEILLES harbour.	
On Ship	27th		Sailed at 7 a.m. Fine and warm.	
"	28		Usual parades. Rained most of the day.	
"	29th		Fine.	
"	30th		Fine. Bathing parades.	
"	31st		Usual parades. Fine and warm.	

1875 Wt. W593/826 1,000,000 4/15 J.B.C. & A. A.D.S.S./Forms/C. 2118.

MESSAGES AND SIGNALS.

TO: 2/East Yorks
1/ K.O.Y.L.I.

Sender's Number: RM 644
Day of Month: 4
AAA

At 4-45 a.m. 4th Oct.15 2/East Yorks Regt. and two coys. 1/K.O.Y.L.I. with one coy. 2/King's Own Regt. attached will assault HOHENZOLLERN REDOUBT. AAA First objective western face of redoubt second objective THE CHORD AAA At 4-15 a.m. artillery will bombard more heavily until 4-45 a.m. when they will lift on to enemy communication trenches AAA When the bombardment commences the first and second line of platoons will get over the parapet advance towards the enemy parapet and lie down AAA Absolute silence

MESSAGES AND SIGNALS.

Prefix	Code	m.	Words	Charge	This message is on a/c of:	Recd. at	m.
Office of Origin and Service Instructions.							
			Sent			Date	
			At	m.	Service.	From	
			To				
			By		(Signature of "Franking Officer.")	By	

TO: 2/East Yorks Regt.
1/ K O Y L I

| Sender's Number. | Day of Month | In reply to Number | |
| RM.644 | 4 | | AAA |

will be maintained until the enemy trench is reached AAA The assault of the CHORD will be undertaken without delay once the REDOUBT has been gained AAA All communication trenches leading from captured works towards the enemy will be filled in and blocked AAA Two sections R.E. will follow behind last platoons and dig communication trenches back from captured work to old British Line AAA Signal Officer 83rd Brigade will arrange the place a telephone on western face of REDOUBT directly

From
Place
Time

The above may be forwarded as now corrected. (Z)

Censor. Signature of Addressee or person authorised to telegraph in his name.

* This line should be erased if not required.
(774-5) — McC. & Co. Ltd., London.— W 1789/1402. 150,000. 8/15. Forms C 2121/10.

MESSAGES AND SIGNALS.

TO	2/ East Yorks Regt. 1/ K.O.Y.L.I.

Sender's Number: RM 644 Day of Month: 4   AAA

it is taken AAA 1/ York & Lancaster Regt. will move up to hold the front British line as it is vacated by 2/ East Yorks and 1/K.O.Y.L.I. AAA Suffolk Regt will be in support trenches behind 1/ York and Lancs Regt AAA 3/8 Surrey Regt. will be at CENTRAL KEEP in reserve

From: 83 Brigade
Time: 1-45 a.m.

B.M. 644 & OPERATION ORDER No. 22.

SECRET   O.O. No 22   Copy No 1
Lt. Col. W^m A Blake D.S.O
Cmdg 2/East Yorkshire Regt
4.10.15

1. Bn will attack WEST FACE of HOHENZOLLERN REDOUBT from point 60 to point 11 at 4.45 a.m. this morning

2. Two platoons of 'B' Coy will form the firing line followed by two platoons in close support and two platoons of D Coy close in rear of them in above order, followed by remaining 2 platoons of that Coy.

3. The first objective will be the WEST FACE, the second objective the chord from point 32 to 60.
On the leading platoon gaining the 1st objective, the supporting platoons will follow through and make good the 2nd objective.

4. Half 'A' Coy with spades will follow in rear of attacking party to consolidate the ~~line~~ position gained. Special attention must be paid to completely blocking all trenches leading towards the enemy

5. Perfect Silence will be observed during the advance.

6. Two squads of bombers will follow with digging party to watch all communication trenches until the blocks have been completed, they will remain on duty there in the vicinity of the blocks with a plentiful supply of bombs

7. Two machine guns will be sent forward with the third two platoons attacking, they will establish themselves in the German line to beat off a counter attack, the remaining guns will be mounted on the front line of trenches and will keep up a steady fire on the enemy's trenches.

8. As the leading company vacates their trenches the supporting companies will move up and take their places, and Y & L will move into their places

9. Every man will carry two sandbags which will be used on improving their trenches directly they have been taken, men should be warned about cutting fire steps and making the

position defensible.
Every man will carry two bombs in his pocket

10. A supply of bombs will be kept close to entrance of communication trench leading to WEST FACE. Bombing Officer will later take steps to ensure that these are sent up quickly.

11. Dressing Station in ~~Central~~ CENTRAL BOYEAU Communication trench

12. Signalling Sergeant will arrange to run out a line to WEST FACE as soon as possible

13. Reports to Battalion Headquarters in front line old English trenches

Issued at   a.m.   O h Cox Lieut
Copy no. 1   War Diary   Adj 2 E York R
        2   A Coy
        3   B "
        4   C
        5   D
        6   Grenadiers
        7   M.G

www.ingramcontent.com/pod-product-compliance
Lightning Source LLC
Chambersburg PA
CBHW081537160426

43191CB00011B/1782